My Mirror
My Reflection
My Depression

My mirror was a reflection of my depression

BY MELISSA MARTIN

My Mirror. My Reflection. My Depression

Copyright © 2022: Melissa Martin

I have tried to recreate events, locales and conversations from my memories of them. In order to maintain their anonymity in some instances I have changed the names of individuals and places, I may have changed some identifying characteristics and details such as physical properties, occupations and places of residence. Some names and identifying details have been changed to protect the privacy of individuals.

First Printed in United Kingdom 2022

Published by Conscious Dreams Publishing
www.consciousdreamspublishing.com

Edited by Daniella Blechner and Elise Abram

Typeset by Oksana Kosovan

ISBN: 978-1-913674-97-7

Contents

Introduction

My mirror was a reflection of my depression. Nevertheless, at the end of my journey, my image and reflection in the mirror was transformed, I started to write this book, as I knew that my experience and story would touch many lives, although I had a traumatic past, my past does not define my future and now my future had a new start. Therefore, I decided to share my story with the world. I want everyone to know that it's possible to have a fresh start and a new beginning after depression, shame, hurt and rejection. Although I knew my story would not be easy to write or share — especially as some areas in my life have never been disclosed before — I was in silent for many years I hid behind my personality, my creativity, my laughs and jokes, but I knew I had to be strong one day, to create my own platform and set the scene for those that are still trapped and hidden in their own story of life. I apologies for not sharing my story a long time ago, but I know that each chapter will inspires and set free at least one person as they read.

Chapter 1

Who is my Audience?

At the beginning of 2019, so many influential and inspirational people died. Nearly every month, there were people posting their losses on social media and this was shocking to me. It also made me reflect upon my life, making me believe that some of these people died with unfulfilled legacies and dreams and they had gone to their graves, their purposes unrealised. Although some of their visions will continue to live on due to 'baton dream transfers', some of these people's dreams and visions will never be known.

As for me, I am still breathing and I still have some life left in me to encourage and support others on their life's journeys. I feel that experiencing real-life traumas over the past 26 years has prepared me to write my book and share my vision to help and support others with their life's journeys as professionals, parents, mothers and wives.

For years, I asked the question, who is my audience? Back in 2017, I started to hold conferences and give talks based on my life's journey, but at the end of each one, I was frustrated because my journey had been filled with so many themes and events I couldn't possibly cover all of them within an hour.

There is a saying: he who knows it feels it. Who better than myself to share my story to help people overcome their life's issues and be the person they were intended to be.

My inspiration

I was inspired to tell my story when I had an encounter with God, and He birthed and unveiled the vision inside of me.

While praying and reading the Bible, I reflected on my life's experiences when I read a story that reminded me of my experience, called 'The Woman at the Well' (John 4).

For years, I was upset with my life and how it was like the story of the woman at the well. In her story, Jesus uncovers her mask and speaks of the things she does in secret; therefore, I knew that one day, I would have to remove my mask and unveil the truth of my abuse, hurt, pain, shame and rejection. The woman at the well had an encounter, an experience with Jesus, but after her encounter, she no longer indulged in her past habits or old behaviours and she gave her life over to God.

I wore my mask for years, until one day while praying, I had an encounter with God. It was then that I felt my last chance to reveal the truth and take off my mask for real. I knew there were people waiting for my arrival and story. Although my journey was a very difficult, painful, lonely process, I trusted God for His perfect timing and worked on my vision by holding conferences based on the woman at the well. I called my conferences 'The Well Experience'. In them, I spoke about my life's experience and had one on one sessions to help and support others on their life's journeys.

The aim of The Well Experience Project was to help people to remove their masks and unveil the truth by coaching, motivating, mentoring and empowering to a life of hope to ensure they accomplished their full potentials. It is in this way that my story would be told.

Chapter 2

Who Am I?

I hated the woman I had become, and I hated my past. I was unable to love myself to full capacity and I never gave my myself the chance to see the beauty within me. I fed myself with lies, telling myself I wasn't good enough, that I was ugly, overweight, always broke, unemployable and I had no achievements, no value and no future. I allowed others to say the same things about me. I also allowed myself to remain hurt and broken and in my 'brokenness', others took advantage by treating me how I felt I should be treated: invisible, rejected, disrespected and used. I had no one to turn to and I felt so alone, but I couldn't stop individuals from abandoning me, but they saw me get up from a low place and stand up tall despite how I felt. I was often numbed with fear, fighting the battle of lies and hurt in my mind, heart and soul.

There was, on the other hand, a set of people who thought I had it all together, but honestly, this woman was a mess most of the time, always wearing a mask, smiling, being the woman these people thought I was. They never knew I was constantly crying inside because I knew I was getting it wrong as a mother, partner, daughter, sister and friend. I felt misunderstood because I didn't always say or do the 'right things'. I was filled with lies, secrets and depression and I had low self-esteem and a lack of confidence, but I also had a smart mouth and that was how I covered my depression I knew how to talk, I knew how to smile, I knew how to say the right things, but most of all, I knew how to wear a mask; it was a mask of scars because I had a history.

Wearing a mask: How easy is it to wear a mask without anyone realising it's an act, but how long can we act? There's always a time when the truth is unveiled. When you watch a movie and you try to identify the bad guy, he usually does something to indicate he is the bad guy, whether at the beginning or the end of the movie, but the truth is that he can't act forever. When all is revealed in the movie, we say, 'I knew it was him!' That's also what we say about people when things go wrong: 'I knew something wasn't quite right with her. She said strange things and I am not surprised she did that.' If this is the case, why don't we say something when there are alarm bells going off? Why don't we step in to help? Is it that our masks are so perfectly fitted that no one can see the gaps? Unfortunately for me, I was hiding, and no one knew. Because I came across as confident and strong, the altogether one who was always smiling, I forever wore my mask to hide my depression, suicidal thoughts, sexual habits, eating habits and broken relationships. I knew how to make what was broken appear fixed. I had the right words for everything because I had studied and worked with those who had depression and how they had worn their masks and I could skilfully do the same. I was so ashamed of my past and I wanted others to believe my story was different. Have you ever gone to a gathering, seen a woman with a family of four — with her husband and two children — who, when she is asked about her life, confidently states she is a business owner, had just bought her first home and sends her children to the best school? Straight away, the listener thinks, 'Wow! What an achievement,' but that's only a story she had told you because of her current situation. What if, when she takes off her mask, she says, 'I used to be a drug addict. I was a teenager mother, but due to my addiction, both of my children are in foster care. I inherited some money from my husband's mum and that's how we got our house, got married and had two more children'? Would your perception of her change? Would you think differently of her? Would you remind her of her past or would you say, 'Well done'?

When you have a traumatic past, even when you have changed, there is always someone who reminds you of your past, forcing you to wear a mask. I saw how people changed their perceptions of me from when I was single to when I got married. There was a different level of respect when I was married, which was awful. I remember going through a divorce and keeping my ring on for ages, masking that I was divorced. When I took pictures, I made sure my ring finger didn't show. I masked the truth, wanting onlookers to see another picture. 'How is your husband?' they would ask. 'He's fine, thanks,' I would reply, although we were separated. I wore a mask, but there was a day coming when it would have to stop; I wanted to stop pretending for myself.

13

Loving without apology

Some people loved me, some liked me and some hated me. I had done some good things in my life, but I have also done some bad things and I learnt to forgive myself, no longer pretending to be someone I was not. I am who I am; every mistake, failure, trial, disappointment, success, joy and achievement has made me the woman I am today. You can love me or not, but if I love you, I will do so with my whole heart and I make no apologies for the way I am. No matter who I meet, be it for a friendship or relationship, I can't help how I love. I give them 100% and I expect the same in return, but unfortunately, this is not always the case. Still, it never changed how I loved, but my kindness was taken for weakness and I gave many people the opportunity to make love seem meaningless though love was important to me. There were times when I met some guys, they asked if I was showing them my true self because I didn't get angry, always loving and caring, as if they wanted to see another me. It was hard for me to mask my love, as I always wanted to be loved, so I would love really hard and expect the same. Although I was hurt many times, showing love before love was given to me, but that's just me. I wore my heart on my sleeve, most men knew I was an easy target and they took what was not theirs and gave nothing in return. After each breakup, I was left with resentment and pain and the next one suffered from the last person's behaviour and it became a vicious cycle. As a result, I would make invasive comments that caused arguments and trust issues and it would be over before it started. I was left with so much love to give and but no one to give it to. So, along my journey, I learnt I couldn't hide my love and loving me had to come first, so I started loving myself.

I became a true fighter. I pushed and pursued. I never gave up. I am not perfect, but I became worthy. I became unstoppable. I was gracefully broken but standing beautifully. I started to love and I was loved by others. I was no longer rejected but transformed. I was filled with love and grace. I became fearless. I dared to win, started to achieve and told myself I would never look back on my past.

Who am I? I am a mother of four, a qualified psychiatric nurse, an author, business owner, an inspirational speaker, a leader, a counsellor, a wife, a mentor and I always strive to be the best version of myself, but my life was not always great. It took me a long time to achieve this status, but every successful goal comes with a test and a fight. How can I explain the pain unless I have felt the pain myself? This book is built on true authenticity, full of emotions and it represents a life cycle of journeys. A part of my journey was silent, but some of it was loud enough for the world to hear and see.

My first journey of pain started in the womb.

– Chapter 3 –

Rejected in the Womb (but Chosen)

I was born on 1 February 1973 around 2:20 a.m.

'Aww… Ms Murphy — it's a beautiful baby girl. Do you still want to sign the adoption papers?' the nurse said. My delivery into the world was my mother's biggest dream as her first daughter had died tragically in a fire when she was a baby.

'No, no, no,' my mother replied, as I slumped on her chest, the umbilical cord still attached. All it would have taken was a snip of the cord and a signature and my whole life would have changed, instead my mum decided to keep her beautiful baby girl.

My mother already had two sons before me, who were five and three and now she was having another child out of wedlock. In those days, being a single parent with three children was shameful as well as stressful.

Where was my dad during these 9 months? That why I stated my rejection started in my mother's womb. When I was eight, my mother used to say to me, 'If you were a boy, the nurse was ready to take you for adoption and I had signed the first set of papers.' To add more drama to this, she said, 'Your father was nowhere to be found because there were rumours that you weren't his child. If she not dark-skinned, then she not Collin's pickney,' so the world — including my father — waited for my arrival to see if I had taken his colour. This meant that I was in the womb, awaiting their approval, acceptance, desire and love. Instead, I was rejected, disowned and unloved by those who knew nothing of my conception.

So, my entrance into life started with rejection, long before I made my first cry when the nurse slapped my bottom to make sure I was breathing. While in my mother's womb, I was covered by a fluid-filled sac. Scientists say this sac is for the baby's protection, but unfortunately, I was not protected from these negative words. I was still being fed through my umbilical cord, but it was with disapproval, lies and my mother's feelings of shame and hurt. My mum was ashamed of being a single mother of two and now she had no partner for her unborn child. She was hurt by others' opinions of others and now she was carrying a child, not knowing whether she was having a boy or girl, whether she would keep it or giving it up, or if she would be with my father or be alone and this caused her to have questions and doubt in her mind. These doubts and those thoughts affected her baby. This was the beginning of traumatic rejection.

Rejection is a big word. It always comes with a NO and sometimes it is very hard to transfer a NO into a YES, especially when someone says, 'No, sorry, you didn't get the job; sorry you have been declined; sorry you can't get the finance for the car; sorry you're ill and we don't have any treatment; and sorry, I am leaving.' Rejection always comes with a NO.

We call cancer the Big C, but I think rejection should be called the Big R because rejection does the same thing as cancer: it eats away every part of who you are, who you want to be and who you want to become. It stops you from going forward and achieving and it keeps you in a web of cycles of fear, hopelessness, regret and/or doubt.

These are our deadly thoughts that go around and around in circles in our minds, just like when someone is hit with cancer. I can't imagine what that might feel like; I have, however, compared this deadly disease with rejection and some will disagree with me. No, I haven't had cancer, but I have heard others speak about how they feel and their thoughts about how it might end, questioning if they will live or die, thinking it was not fair, asking why me? I have watched family members and friends who had cancer and how they quickly deteriorated, even after all of the chemotherapy treatments. You can be all in the clear one minute and the next, it comes back again, but this time, it can lead to death. This is just like rejection — you don't know what incident or experience will be linked to you going back to a place of rejection, leading you to an experience that feels like death.

No one really likes to talk about death, but when you're going through a life-threatening illness, your life is put on hold and all you can see is your coffin, your funeral and the words from your family in your eulogy. That is how rejection made me feel. I had a near-death experience; this is the only way I can describe the experience. I was alive but in a coffin. Have you ever seen those movies when someone is buried alive and they bang on the coffin door, shouting, 'Let me out of here! I'm alive!'? Well, that was me. I was shouting from inside a coffin that I was alive and not dead, but I was encircled by fear and doubt and the feelings of rejection kept me in place and unable to move forward or achieve or complete the things I had started. Instead, I heard the voices telling me it was too late, I should have, I was too old, I wasn't educated, and I would never become anything.

It was not until I was about 30 years old when I first experienced feelings of rejection and I understood that rejection was serious enough to keep me stagnating, lifeless and feeling almost dead. I remember when I was preparing for my second marriage and I had an encounter with God. He gave me the revelation that my rejection had begun inside the womb and I was still carrying those feelings from the womb and all the hurt and pain from my broken relationships with past partners, friends and family. I had never given myself the opportunity to forgive and accept; therefore, I had not closed those chapters and I was still carrying the hurt, wearing a mask, saying one thing but feeling something else in my heart. I found it so hard to express how I felt, and I lived like that for years. I could not close those chapters because I didn't want to accept what had happened to me and how people had made me feel. I could not change what happened to me, but I wanted apologies and to confront each person who had done me wrong. I knew that even if I asked them the question of why, it would be pointless, so I never did. Instead, I learnt that acceptance is closure. The day I began to forgive, accept and forgive myself was the day I headed in the right direction, taking small steps toward healing. I only realised later down the road that I was not totally healed.

When I met my second husband, he was so loving, always wanting to hold my hand, give me hugs and show appreciation in his expression of his love. It was then I realised that I could not relate to those types of expressions because I had not seen or felt this in my previous relationships. I found it difficult to receive love from my husband because I was scared it was just a show and he didn't really mean it. This could be because, in the past, I had men who would say one thing, but their actions did something else. I, therefore, believed that something bad was going to happen and I was waiting for him to reject me because that was what I was used to. For a long time, I allowed rejection to rule me and dictate who I was and where I was going. I allowed that fear of rejection to cripple my mind and keep me isolated. I allowed rejection to play mind games with me, especially with the important male figures in my life. Rejection told me my father was embarrassed by me because my life was a mess, I had children out of wedlock, and I had no career.

These thoughts made me distant as a result of the shame. Rejection told me that my son was upset with the men I had brought into his life to father him because they were not the best choices and this interfered with our mother/son relationship, so I couldn't embrace him as a mother should. Rejection told me that my Spiritual Father was disappointed in the choices I made, and he was upset with me. With all these thoughts, how could I allow another male figure to come into my life as a husband? I was frightened of my past experiences — love me today and reject me tomorrow, make promises then break them, speak well of me, then put me down — these thoughts ruled me for years. I allowed rejection to become a part of my life and I felt like I was wearing the word 'rejection' on my forehead. My thoughts of rejection made me feel depressed, isolated, fearful, lifeless and worthless. In this lowest time in my life, I forgot my value. I forgot who I was. Instead, I was haunted by my past experiences and bad choices. Now, I was being given a second chance to love again, and I didn't want to bring those thoughts into my marriage because I had carried the baggage of hurt for years. Although I had taken small steps to let go of the suitcase and wardrobes of hurt, I still had a few carrier bags, so I had to have a conversation with those who were important to me. This way, I could feel totally free and be confident enough to marry a male figure without thinking that men were all the same. It was not my husband's fault that I had made bad decisions and choices in life. He had just arrived to bring me love, to show me that I didn't have to stay rejected by the men who had claimed to love me before.

For many years, I blamed my father for not being there for me when I was a child, not embracing me with a father's love and letting me know how beautiful I was. When I became a teenager, I tried to find that 'father's love' in men because I did not know how I should be loved or treated by men, So when I started having relationships, I had no clue what to expect. Every relationship ended in brokenness, but it wasn't their faults. I was looking for a particular type of love and that wasn't the boyfriend-type of love — it was a father's love for which I looked. I wanted to be fathered. Today, I know that my dad loves me dearly, but during my childhood, he wasn't home enough to express it as he was always working.

What was my definition of a father's love? I didn't know what I needed or wanted, but when I looked at friends and they expressed how their fathers treated them, I thought from their experiences that this is what love was. So, I used to compare what they had experienced from their fathers, with my father, but it was nowhere near the same, so this left me angry and I lived with unforgiveness towards my father for many years, I was trapped, distant and I sabotaged all my relationships. When things went wrong in my relationships, I would revert back to that pain. It was the pain of rejection in the womb, but I had blamed my past relationships for the hurt I had experienced in the womb. I kept hearing those self-blaming thoughts: *no one loves me, I shouldn't be here, the world would be a better place without me, why was I born?* It was then I realised that the rejection from all those years, from birth to 45-years-old, was a reflection of my experience in the womb. All of those hidden feelings had turned into hurt, pain and misunderstanding and lead me into a depression I didn't know I had.

Chapter 4

Depression Hidden

What is depression? To me, it was a word that was never used in the mouths of my culturally Black family background. Nope, it was forbidden, especially in my house. Because of the Black community into which I was born, we were all known as strong Black men and women who could fight anything, we didn't lose; we always won, we used our masks as our defense mechanisms to prove to society that we were fighters due to our history of slavery and racism. Either that or we were a group of hidden people, filled with untold stories of hurt, too ashamed of our pasts, who used our fighting spirits to look normal and strong. Growing up, I noticed that even if we didn't have the best jobs, houses, or cars, or have loads of money, we all believed in one thing: we were great fighters and survivors.

Madison Grey, author of *Depression, the Other Side of 'Man Up'*, echoes these sentiments and discusses potential pitfalls:

'For Black men, we are taught to not deal with our feelings. Yeah, that's true. I even told myself to 'man up' last weekend, but then I wondered how many times I had flown off the handle when I kept it all bottled in rather than talking about it. If that's the case, how many men turned their depression into anger, resulting in violence? How many lives could have been saved, caps and gowns been worn, or prison beds left unoccupied if brothers just had the chance to open up?'

A lack of the acceptance of Black men expressing their emotions is a hurdle to Black men receiving treatment for depression. Black women are tormented by similar issues because they don't want to be seen as weak.

Moreover, according to the National Health Service website (2019), sometimes, there's a trigger for depression, such as life-changing events like bereavement, but you can also become depressed for no obvious causes. Depression is common and can affects about one in ten people at some point in their lives. It also affects men and women, both young and old.

I first saw depression in my home as a child when, sadly, one of my baby brothers passed away at the age of two. My mother had no coping strategies, nor did she have any idea that she had not only lost her lovely son, but she had lost her other seven children, too, because my memory from that time was my mum, appeared absent, unbothered, non-engaged, angry, frustrated, isolated and neglectful. In those days, I didn't know this was depression! My mother faced depression and anxiety through no fault of her own, but this tragic event messed up my family home, leaving me with two parents who were never there.

Sadly, depression can also be inherited from your parents. NHS states: 'people with a family history of depression are more likely to experience it themselves' ('NHS 2019').

Unveiling depression

I hated the side of me that shuts down, says goodbye without questioning, walks out of relationships and friendships without apologies, agrees to call or meet up but disappoints others and makes excuses for my failed promises. This is when my past flashed before my face and I don't feel like living. I automatically die inside and wanted to live in a coffin. My anxiety and fears take over, and I wanted out of this troubled life. No one knew I was suffering from depression until today and they will know once they have read my book. How do you stay true to yourself when everyone has an opinion? How do you tune out all the noise and be true to who you really are?

No, not me — I couldn't have depression. I was becoming a nurse, I was a mother, a wife and a mentor, so this couldn't happen to me. All I could do is block out the symptoms of depression and stay in my coffin and bang quietly on the lid, so quietly that no one would hear me banging but myself. I wanted to come out, but I didn't know how. I knew that sadness, exhaustion, unhappiness, anger, irritability, frustration, a loss of interest in pleasurable or fun activities, sleep issues, no energy, craving unhealthy foods, anxiety and isolation were symptoms of depression, but I chose to live with the symptoms because I feared others' opinions, like those of my work colleagues, friends and family. I also feared what my brothers and sisters in my church might say. They were the ones I really couldn't tell because they would say, 'That is a demon. It is not of God.' So, I continued to wear a mask and live with my depression. Most people are ashamed to own the stigma and label that comes with depression. As a Christian, I heard this term from my brother and sisters in Christ. I call it Christian jargon: 'I might be going through, but God is with me and I am just holding on.' So, I kept silent and I was ashamed of my issues.

I remember people used to say to me, 'You're just like your mum. You really look like your mum,' but I used to get upset because I used to associate my mother with depression and anxiety and I saw myself as the opposite, but that was my prideful thoughts and my hidden mask, when I was exactly that: I was my mother. I was facing depression.

Black women are expected to be strong in a way that makes them the 'mules' of the community. They are expected to carry the burden when others can't, so they find themselves risking their health to be the shoulders everyone leans on. It's a burden they feel obligated to carry. Josie Pickens captured this sentiment in an article in *Ebony* entitled *Depression and the Black Superwoman Syndrome*. Pickens wrote:

'I honestly believe we're so accustomed to delivering the strong Black woman speech to ourselves and everyone else that we lose our ability to connect to our humanness and thus our frailty. We become afraid to admit that we are hurting and struggling, because we fear that we will be seen as weak. And we can't be weak. We've spent our lives witnessing our mothers and their mothers be strong and sturdy, like rocks. We want to be rocks.'

The first time I knew I was depressed was when I was listening to a client expressing why she feels depressed and as she spoke, it was like I was looking in a mirror and I was the reflection of what she was saying. She said, 'My husband is cheating on me and it hurts so much. I have children and I can't do anything with them because I have turned to alcohol to suppress my feelings. I don't know what to do. I can't tell my family and friends. Please, help me.' I smiled superficially and allowed the other nurse to advise her because I needed answers, too. As I left work that evening, I got into my car and screamed with tears, broke down and shouted, 'I am depressed...I am depressed!'

My tears were uncontrollable. It was then I knew I suffered from depression. I describe it as 'a depressive mask'. I was depressed but smiling, depressed but praying for people, depressed but advising, depressed but counselling, depressed but being a mother, depressed but studying and depressed but speaking my dream. I had no choice but to wear my depressive mask as I wanted to protect my children. I had already failed them, having them at a young age and bringing them up on my own. At the age of 23, I already had three children from three different men, and I had no man beside me. All I wanted was a man to help and support me with my children, or should I say, to help me with my bad choices of men. I believed at the time that these men wanted to make life with me, only to find out later that they had different agendas and motives and that ended up in broken relationships.

As I was no longer with either of their fathers, my children had to go through their own insecurities and the rejection of single parenthood. Therefore, I couldn't allow my depression to stop me from being a mother. Even though I don't think I was the best mother, I fought and pushed to fulfil my dreams for my children. I wanted to combat the stigma of being a single parent. I wanted my children to see my achievements. Despite my rough start, I wanted a great finish so they could see that you can do all things and never ever give up on achieving your dreams, even when life seems a mess. How could I let my depression stop me? There was still something in me, fighting, but unfortunately, I had made another bad choice and my ex partner had mentally abused me and robbed me of that little bit of fight, building insecurities in me.

From his words, I instilled low self-esteem in myself and I lost my worth and value. He lied and deceived me. He was unfaithful and my role in our union was stolen. I was so lonely; I had no hope and no one to turn to. I had waited so long for a commitment with a man who would help and support me with my children and now my 'solid relationship' was crumbling away. I had lost all trust and I hated the feeling of being trapped, but I stayed in the relationship because my pride kept me there and because of shame that I would face from naysayers who would say, 'I told you so.' The longer I stayed in that relationship, the more I was ruined, and it was killing me inside. All I could do was turn to alcohol, as it helped me to suppress my feelings. While drinking, I often had moments of happiness, then a moment of tears. Although I was living a Christian life, I wore a mask of lies. I was a total mess and I had reverted secretly back to my old ways.

I was still going to church, but I masked my drinking. No one knew I was secretly drinking every day. It got so bad that I would buy a can of Coke and little shots of brandy and walk up and down the main road so I could drink with no one knowing. Then, before going home, I would buy a bottle of wine to drink with my dinner. To my family, it seemed okay to have a glass of wine with my meal, but what they didn't know is that the wine was a top-up to keep me suppressed and face the man who was crippling my mind. Unfortunately, I was caught in a web of lies that drinking alcohol was my only option, but at the time, it was the only way I knew how to cope. Alcohol became my coping mechanism. I became confident when I drank because I lost myself.

At the time, I couldn't turn to the church as they were not in agreement with my choice for a relationship. I couldn't go to my family because I wanted to protect my relationship with him in case things would change with us. I didn't want my family to say, 'How can you stay after what he has done?' so I stayed silent and depressed for three more years. I looked to God for change, but the more I stayed, the worse it got. My happiness was being robbed and my achievements were being delayed.

One day, I asked my mother if she was happy that she stayed in her marriage despite the initial affair my father had before they were married. She started to cry and said, 'Yes, I love your dad,' but I heard a 'NO!' and a hint of regret. It was then I decided that I had the opportunity to leave my ex-partner and I still had some time to be happy but looking for love is not always easy.

Chapter 5

Looking for Love in all the Wrong Places

How could I find love when I had no idea what love was? I thought love was having children with men. I thought I was privileged that these men had wanted me to carry their child. Why was my perception of love so distorted? Was it because I did not respect myself, know my worth, or know my value? Was it the sexual abuse I had experienced as a child? No one, including my parents to this day, knew how dirty, unclean and ashamed I felt. I told no one that, on several occasions, the husband of a family friend had taken my innocence. He bribed me with money, called me into his room and touched me in areas that felt unusual to me. He always gave me a gesture with his eyes to go upstairs and he would put his finger on his mouth for me to be quiet. Because I wanted the money for sweeties, I allowed him to lift my dress up, pull my knickers down, and push himself into me, while my mother spoke with his wife downstairs. Was this the start of being unvalued, worthless, or feeling dirty? I blamed myself for years because I was greedy for money and I thought I deserved it. I have lived with the self-blame forever and no one knew because I thought I would be told that I was just as bad because I had taken the man's money. I kept it to myself and I battled with it for years because it was not worth talking about. I am all grown up now and I didn't know he was my perpetrator until it was too late. My teenage life was a mess because my childhood started as a mess. I buried this abuse for years because it was easier. Even now, as I write, I want to delete these words and never talk about it. I just want to take this pain to my grave. Tears running down my face as I write. I have an inner silence — silent secrets — and in this silence, I was reminded that I've been seated on the opposite side of depression for years, listening to others speak of their abuse, depression, rape and hurt and not being able to break my own silence. Listening, advising, ministering, mentoring and speaking to those people, but at the same time, I needed to hear it for myself. Isn't it amazing how we can give advice to others, but we can't face our own demons? I know there are many people like myself — professionals, leaders, young and old — who face this same silence, unable to break their own silence, but who continue to support and help others to overcome their ordeals, while continuing to sit opposite depression. I used to listen to men and woman who had publicly come out about their ordeals of rape and abuse. I used to think they were so brave and I could never express that. However, going through my abuse made me stay silent. 'Shhh...don't tell your mum; she will say it's your fault', 'Don't tell no one, or you won't get no more money', 'I am the only one that loves you' — these are some of the lies abusers speak into your ears and you are made to believe it is the truth. I was robbed, deceived, corrupted and I remained silent and I never had the guts to speak out. I have been stuck for years because I thought I deserved to be abused because of my love of money.

The abuse opened my desire for sex. My innocence was taken away and sex became addictive and I needed to fulfil this feeling, so I became promiscuous. I allowed anyone to take my body. For years, I wanted to know if it was just me wanting sex or if it was others taking advantage of me and abusing my dignity. I remember staying over at a family friend's home and at one time or another, someone wanted to fondle my private parts or have sex with me. It got so bad that I couldn't wait to stay at some of these people's houses as I knew what I was going to get. I wanted it, and now I needed it because I was addicted — addicted to sexual abuse!

It became like a drug and I needed my fix. It got so bad that I thought, let's step it up a bit and bring new people into my addiction, such as girls I would watch pornography of women and masturbate, I wouldn't class myself as a lesbian, but I was addicted to sex and not an individual, so if I could just reach a climax, anyone would do. For years, I thought I had SEX written on my forehead. Everywhere I went, I had some kind of sexual encounter with someone. I didn't know how I would break free from this addiction. All I wanted was sex without a relationship, so when I found one that ticked all the boxes and he wanted the same thing, no strings attached, he would be my sex partner until I was bored. Then, I would move. Sometimes

I would go back if I was not being fulfilled by my new sex partner. I became a professional at this game, and I knew how to lure new and old people back into my bed. Was I a secret prostitute?

This had all started when one man had taken my innocence as a child, taken away my opportunity to live a normal life, setting me up to become a sex addict instead. When I turned 16-years-old, there was nothing I had not experienced or done with boys, but I was wearing a mask. When I was 11-years-old, friends at school used to ask me, 'Have you lost your virginity yet?' I would reply, 'No,' knowing full well that I lost it at the age of six years old.

I remember that I was around 14-years-old and a family friend came over to my mother's house. I was the only person in the house, and he started groping me and making sexual advances. Although I had a lot of experience, I was also scared because he was a couple of years older. In some way, I loved the experience and I was already addicted to sex, so I allowed him to continue. I remember bleeding. It was then that I thought I was all grown up and I was happy because I was ready for the big boys and my sex life would go to the next level. I started bragging to my friends at school that I had lost my virginity. At that point, it felt normal because most girls had boyfriends or were having sex, but the truth of the matter was that although I felt dirty and my inner body was a mess from the time I was a child, it was okay to tell the world I had started to have sex at the age of 14-years-old. Then again, I was broken and filthy.

Though I had been broken for years, I knew I deserved more than sex, but I equated having sex and getting money as a part of being loved as this was what my first perpetrator had led me to believe. Having sex meant that someone loved me and receiving money was an exchange for sex.

How would I meet a real boyfriend who loved me for me and not just sex, someone who valued me and wanted more than sexual benefits, not just friends with benefits, but real romance like you see in the movies? While writing this book, I watched a movie called 'Addicted', based on a woman who was abused as a child. Although she moved on to get married and have children, she was addicted to sex and her husband could not fulfil her needs, so she went out and slept with other men to fulfil her childhood addiction of abuse. She had to go through counselling to accept that this addiction was not because she didn't want to be loved or she didn't want to be with her husband, or because she wanted to cheat on him. Rather it was purely based on her abuse as a child and the feeling had continued into her adult life. During her counselling, she had to accept that her abuser had caused her addiction and it was then that she could close her chapter. Acceptance is closure. How would I accept that what I had gone through was okay when I hadn't spoken to anyone about it? All they could see was the evidence of my broken relationships, but they did not know the underlying issue of why all my children had different fathers. I had no clear pathway, but unfortunately, the beginning of my abuse reflected what I was going to be.

My life became messier and messier as the years went by after falling pregnant at the age of 17. Everyone could see that I could not hold down a relationship and I was being blamed for having babies and not securing my life with any ambition or stability. How can you be stable if you don't know what stability feels like? All I knew was that having sex with me meant that they loved me, as did having their babies. I should be privileged to carry their children because my inner emotions said, 'Why would anyone want me when I am so dirty inside?' It was okay to let anyone have me because my life had already gone bad — how could I change something that had begun without my consent? If they knew that I was fighting a battle inside with depression, anger and worthlessness, then they would understand why I kept making these mistakes. I was misunderstood.

Chapter 6

Misunderstood as a Woman

Sometimes, women can be misunderstood and it's clear that society, religion and culture pigeon-hole women in their perspective of how women should be seen. In some cultures, if a woman argues with her man and he punches her, he isn't in the wrong, but if she's been hurt, his family would support him and tell the woman to be quiet, respectful and accept an apology; however, if she had done the same, his family would tell her she has no respect and she is out of order because she is a woman and women don't have the right to be angry, nor are they equal to men. So, the degree of a woman's innocence is directly related to the degree of a woman's silence and she must face the man's oppression and abuse. If a woman's husband cheated on her, she must tolerate his bad behaviour to save her marriage and listen to the stupid excuse that it's in their nature to cheat. Instead, a woman should lose weight, look good, keep the house together, pray harder and be more pleasing; however, if a woman cheated, she would be called a 'whore', she would have no right to look elsewhere for love and emotional support and she would be called an irresponsible mother. If a man lost his wife to death and remarried after a year, he would be congratulated and praised for moving on as he needs a wife to look after him, but if a woman loses her husband to death and remarries after four years, people would say it's too soon. They might even question if she was sleeping with the same man when her husband was alive.

As women, we have been given a role of huge responsibility to prove that we have the right to live a certain way and if we get things wrong, we are put into boxes of negativity. I, too, was misunderstood. I was lost in my family's house, filled with seven brothers and me, the only girl. As the girl, the expectation was that I should be like a girl and not a boy, but I enjoyed marbles, action figures and fighting, rather than being a princess with baby dolls. Was that because I thought I was not a pretty princess because I was ugly inside, filled with lies, filth and deceit? I was misunderstood with my silent secrets. There were times my mother would say that I was dirty and didn't like washing, but I thought: why should I clean myself when I am only going to be dirty again with abuse? I thought that if I stayed dirty, my abusers would not want to go there, but that didn't matter or stop them. Why didn't my mother know? Why didn't she read the signs? How come she couldn't read the signs? My knickers were always filthy and I used to wet the bed, but she just thought I was dirty and I didn't want to wash. These were the alarm bells indicating that I was being abused. I don't want to blame my mum for not recognising the signs, as in those days, mental health was not a thing. I remember being taken to the doctor's one day when I couldn't stop laughing. I laughed at everything, even if it was a serious moment. What did that laugh look like? I would shake my head, leaning it back and forth while laughing hysterically. The laugh was one that should have indicated I was mentally unwell. I remember family members talking about me, thinking I couldn't hear them. One of them said I was acting 'maddy-maddy'. In other words, I was acting as if I were mad, but my laugh was a scream for help. I wasn't mad — my laugh was my tears. This shows how easy it is to misunderstand signs of abuse for something else, how we overlook the real issue and judge what we think it might be. I had many incidents in my life where I was misunderstood in which my past hurts played a big role. This was why I did certain things that made no sense to others; I was misunderstood.

*****

When I got married the first time, it was mainly because I was trying to get back at my ex. My ex had bought me an engagement ring, made me wait for years, then broke up with me without keeping his promise, so I wanted to prove to him that someone else loved me and I was worth marrying. The outside world would say, 'How could you marry someone so quickly?' but I was misunderstood for my actions as the underlying issue was a lack of forgiveness, shame and hurt.

While battling with depression for years, no one knew why I didn't turn up to friends' and family functions, but I was misunderstood. They thought I was selfish, keeping to myself, religious, or had no money, but the truth is that it was my depression, which would not allow me to dress up, eat sensibly, value myself, or socialise; therefore, I would find every excuse. When I looked in the mirror, I saw ugly, dirty, filthy and fat, a wall disguised with lies and deceit. Sometimes, I would reject phone calls as I did not want to be confronted with the 'whys' or the questions of why I hadn't turned up or why I hadn't answered their calls. After a while, my social relationships and friendships broke down and I had no control over my actions as my depression controlled me. I was afraid I might say things buried deep down inside of me. There a scripture in the Bible that says, 'Out of your mouth, the abundance of your heart speaks,' and I wasn't ready to break my silence. Staying away and not going out was much easier, as I didn't want what was buried to come out, especially after having a social drink of alcohol. I knew that the deep-rooted hurt in my heart would come out one day and I knew that one day, the wrong person might suffer my anger and I wanted to protect my friends and family.

I went through repeated cycles for years. I used to start things and not finish them. My depression was hidden from everyone. I had bouts of happiness, then cycles of depression. When I was depressed, I ate myself to sleep. Once, I put on three stone in one month after the man I loved left me. The reason I was so depressed was because I thought I had finally found someone who had loved me for who I was, along with my three children out of wedlock and that he respected me as a woman as he built up my confidence and always reminded me of my worth. When he left, I felt used and deceived and like no one really loved me — who could really want me with my three children? So, rejection kicked in again.

*****

It is hard when you see people behaving in a strange way, but sometimes, it is an indication there is a problem, and it should not be misunderstood. I used to wish that someone, somewhere, would rescue me and say, 'Don't do that, don't go there,' but instead, I had to face these traumatic issues alone. Was it because I was a woman and we are men's backbones? Or was it because I looked okay? Was it because I kept silent? Or was it because I was misunderstood? All of this misunderstanding turned food into my barrier and the big, beautiful me became the big, ugly.

Chapter 7

Food, Love and My Body

Loving me was so hard. When I looked in the mirror, what did I see? Ugly, fat, lies, low self-esteem, lack of confidence, hurt and pain. What should I have seen? Beauty, smiles, love, joy, confidence and inspiration. I would hear people's accolades of honour, greatness, confidence and beauty where I was concerned, but I masked my depression and the only thing keeping me going was my relationship with food. I abused food, but it was my escape into happiness. Eating felt like a reward and when things went wrong in relationships, I comforted and rewarded myself with food when there was an argument or break-up. This was my way of saying, 'Don't worry, hun, you are appreciated,' but unfortunately, food had become my barrier. My weight went up and down. On my good days, I was the same weight and on my bad days, my weight could spike up to two or three stones. This caused low self-esteem, a lack of confidence, avoidance, unhealthy relationships and my inability to love myself. I hated when people said, 'You look so beautiful. You always look so nice,' especially the times when I battled my ugly ME moments. At times, I couldn't even look in the mirror, especially when my weight had shot up. I wouldn't weigh myself, but my face and clothes were the evidence that I had fallen into that vicious cycle. All that time, I never realised I had an eating disorder until I started working with eating disorder patients. That was another moment when I sat in the opposite seat, dealing with my mental health. When patients started describing the depths of their illnesses, I recognised that I had a problem. It was a problem I could not solve, so I overlooked it and continued to abuse my body. My food was my defence, my comfort zone, my barrier and my control. I could not control my situation, but I could control what I ate, and my lack of control was getting out of hand. I ate everything and anything. I would eat in secret, so no one knew I wasn't eating properly. I would eat at home and go out to pretend I was going to the local shops, but really, I went to a takeaway restaurant — McD's drive thru was my special friend — and I would order two Happy Meals. I remember eating it fast in my car, so I could quickly dispose of the evidence, but then, I bought treats to take home — chocolates, sweets, biscuits, crisps and fizzy drinks. This looked normal to everyone but going to the local shops was just another cover-up to go out so I could indulge in my secret comfort eating. I was living a lie and a deadly secret when overeating. Family members made remarks about my weight gain, but I was in denial. I would say that I wasn't eating much, and I wasn't sure why I had put on the weight, but inside, I grappled with denial and was screaming for help. As I got bigger, I destroyed myself and those around me. I was angry with myself and I became unsociable and couldn't commit to anything as I lacked confidence.

In one relationship, I was mentally abused about my weight and the more I was abused, the more I ate. The way he looked at me with disgust made me retreat into my shell. It was a shell of shame, insecurity, and low self-esteem. He wouldn't take me out, go to family functions, or let me be around his friends. After a while, he disclosed that he was ashamed of my weight and he couldn't bring himself to go places with me. Because he was so ashamed of me, I thought that if I ate more, I would get bigger and then he would be more ashamed. I wanted to get back at him and make him more embarrassed, so I started to self-sabotage and kept eating until I was unrecognisable. I reached my heaviest weight and I was dying inside. I had thoughts of harming myself. I wanted to use a knife to burst my stomach. I wanted to have that deflated feeling, a bit like sticking a pin in a balloon so it would burst and deflate. I had the notion that I would lose weight by doing this. I joined every weight loss group, but that only lasted for a few weeks. When I saw a little bit of weight loss, I would think it was okay to eat normally, so I indulged in my old habits again, especially when things got worse in my relationship when it was my way of seeking comfort. I remember my son saying to me, 'Mum, don't think about your weight. Just dress up in nice clothes and people will see your clothes and not your weight,' but my thoughts had got out of hand and the opinions of others were slowly destroying me.

Suicidal thoughts

I secretly wanted to be dead. I could no longer look in the mirror and look at myself and I wanted out. I remember being on holiday, being in the shopping centre, looking over the balcony and imagining myself splattered on the ground. I never heard voices or had any real intention of killing myself, but I wanted to do something to stop the feelings I was having. At that very moment, seeing myself on the ground seemed like an easy way to escape, but then I remembered those I would be leaving behind, especially my children. I imagined the news report would say, 'A woman in her forties on holiday from England sadly took her life. Her family is in anguish at her loss,' and I quickly zoned out of my thoughts and tried to enjoy my holiday. I had that thought when I went shopping and I would pass a mirror, walk back, do a double-take and be in shock at how big I was because inside, I felt the same, but the mirror was saying something else. Several times, when I went on the train, I had thoughts of jumping. It was so bad that I nearly had a panic attack and I wanted the train to come quickly so I could get on before I jumped. It was the weirdest feeling. I could see myself jump, but luckily, I didn't hear a voice pushing me to follow it through. Several times, I had to speak the word of God and pray for my life, as it is definitely not normal for Christian women to have these thoughts. If I told the Church I was feeling suicidal, I would need deliverance. If I told my family, I would need sectioning in a hospital. These feelings were only thoughts and I had to pray my way out of them. How strange is it that you can inspire others around you, counsel people and advise people to do the right thing, but you, yourself, needs the same counselling and encouragement? I struggled with these thoughts of rejection and being overweight at my lowest times. I had to start distracting myself by thinking about the positive things in my life: my children, grandchildren, parents, family and goals. I needed to combat the battle and look in the mirror.

Chapter 8

My Mirror

The term 'my mirror' reflects what only I can see in the mirror, the battles and my thoughts of my image. I struggled to like what I saw, and I saw UGLY. Looking in the mirror is a scary experience when you have low self-esteem, a lack of confidence and feel like you have no self-worth. It's difficult, as some mirrors can make you look much bigger or slimmer and sometimes, you can look really beautiful or even ugly. I always wondered why different mirrors gave me a different look, especially when I thought I looked smaller and someone would say, 'Oh, you look like you put on some weight.' Was my mirror deceiving me, or was I listening to the opinions of others again? Were my past insecurities playing tricks on my mind? I realised that every mirror produced a different image, depending on the lighting, size, quality and surroundings in the room. There are so many factors why you might look different in a mirror and there was no real answer for me. I allowed others' words to dictate what I saw in the mirror because I was so used to hearing negativity about my weight, my clothes and my image until I believed what was being said about me and it felt true. When I looked in the mirror, I saw others' words in my reflection. If someone said to me, 'You look big, untidy and not yourself,' I believed them though I hadn't looked in the mirror because I was accustomed to hearing negative words from my childhood right up into adulthood, causing me to accept what was said. My mirror always looked broken and my image was constantly distorted, ugly and unfixable. As we all know, it is hard to put a broken mirror back together and a broken mirror loses its value to reflect an image. Just like a broken mirror, I had lost my value, my ability to be better and my ability to become. Instead, I was riddled with thoughts that told me there was no point in looking nice, as who would want me? Who would love my past? Who would see my value?

What is interesting is the value of money. When you scrunch up a 50-pound note, step on it, or even slightly tear it, although it been through so many changes and can be almost destroyed, the value of the money remains the same and it can still be used for the purpose for which it was made. Therefore, the purpose of my life was still valuable, regardless of what I felt or what I had experienced. As we all know, different mirrors produce different images, so I had to change the mirror into which I was looking and that meant changing my surroundings, friends and conversations. The question was, how would I get to that place of change? How could I see another image when all I could see was the reflection of others' words? Over the years, I had created so many insecurities inside my head.

When I started taking vocal lessons, my tutor told me to look in the mirror and watch my expressions as I sang, but when I looked in the mirror during vocal training, I broke down into tears. I couldn't see my beauty or worth in the mirror. All I saw was ugliness, pain, hurt, rejection and guilt. That was when I identified that I had lost my confidence which interfered with my dreams and visions. The power of the words had taken over my mind and I was stuck.

Although I was stuck, I noticed there was a set of people who would see my heart and my accomplishments rather than my outward appearance and those people would speak life-changing words that would help change my thoughts about what I looked like and how I felt. Although I heard a lot of negativity, I also heard the words of those who reminded me of who I really was. At first, I didn't hear what they had said, let alone feel what they said, but each time I heard something positive, it changed my thoughts and transformed my beliefs. The ugly images in my head were turning to beauty! I shifted my thoughts and was on a journey of self-affirmation.

One day, while at university, I saw a colleague that worked on my nursing ward. She had never seen me in my own clothes as I was always in my nurse's uniform and when she saw me, she said, 'Wow! Is that how you look out of your nurse's uniform? You make slims girls want to be BIG.' It was these words that allowed me to re-visit the mirror. I wanted to see what she saw. I hadn't looked in the mirror for ages, but now, my experience with the mirror was different; I wanted a mirror transformation.

51

Who do I see? A new girl, a new me, but it took me a long time to see who I was and what I really looked like until I removed my mask. I was hidden for a long time, always smiling but dying inside and it took me a long time before I was ready to reveal who I really was. I decided to try the mirror experiment, literally looking into the mirror and speaking words of positive affirmation. I spoke life into my dead reflection.

– Chapter 9 –

My Reflection

A reflection is an image seen in a mirror. Another form of reflection is 'the process of internally examining and exploring an issue of concern, triggered by an experience, which creates and clarifies meaning in terms of self and which results in a changed conceptual perspective' (Boyd and Fales). My experience of my reflection was exactly that. When I looked in the mirror, I saw an image and I reflected on what I used to look like and how I looked now, examining my image in my head, knowing that this was not what I used to be or used to look like? The experience triggered my emotions and the emotions triggered me to reflect on my image. When you are mentally abused about your weight, and you use food for comfort, it becomes a repeated cycle. I hated what I saw, but I also hated what I heard from my abuser. The more I ate, the more my reflection in the mirror changed for the worse, and the abuse continued because my perpetrator did not see a change in my image.

Although I was overweight and the mirror confirmed this reflection, my weight gain was his excuse. I was overweight and he was entitled to look for someone else because I wasn't his type anymore. I would find receipts in his pockets from Ann Summers for underwear, sized 10 to 12. This, obviously, wasn't my size and he was giving someone else what he should have been giving to me. This made me feel worse and I was dying of jealously. I wanted to be a size 12. I wanted that underwear. I used to wonder what she looked like. Was she pretty? What was her complexion? How did she make him feel? I wanted what she was getting. Although I had the status of being his main woman, the roles were reversed, and I was like his side-chick. It was like when the side-chick works extra-hard to get the status of being the main woman and she has to do everything in her power for him to love her like his main women, but she didn't have to work for my status, because she had him and I had lost him. I wanted him back. I wanted him to love me for who I was. I wanted him not to see my outward appearance. I wanted a chance to be loved, but he never saw the woman he first met. My weight was getting out of control and I was getting bigger and my pain was getting deeper and there was no turning back. I didn't have the willpower to change my image or how I felt because I was depressed.

Chapter 10

My Depression

My depression — or what I define as being 'my depression' — is based on how I felt and my experience rather than depression in clinical terms or what I saw from other people's experiences. It was my depression. Although I was not clinically diagnosed with depression, I knew I wasn't well, and I needed help. I was forced not to deal with my depression as I was Black, a mother, a wife, a student nurse, a leader, a mentor and lastly a Christian. How could I tell someone I was depressed when the odds were against me? I remember telling a family member that I was depressed, and they stated there was no such thing as depression.

I would dare not express this to my Christian brother or sister, as I would just be told to pray and that depression was a spirit from the devil. I couldn't speak to my university as I thought I would have my course taken away, especially because I was already fighting to stay with the course as I'd had some personal interruptions and challenges. This course wasn't just any course — it was mental health degree and I wondered how I could be facing depression when I was studying to have a positive impact on those who were dealing with mental health issues. This was why I needed to wear a mask to complete my course and look like a winner and I knew how to wear my mask well.

As a Black family, we are taught not to share our feelings with our children as this will cause them to lose respect and make them feel as if they are on the same level as their parents, so I had to suffer in silence and pretend I was okay. Depression affected my family and me. It affected my relationship with my children because, to them, it looked like I didn't care. The truth was that I was suffering from depression and silently struggling to be a good mum and although I was often absent and they spent a lot of time with my parents, that was my way of dealing with my depression and I couldn't cope with the reality that I had three small people for whom I was responsible. I carried the shame of my past broken relationships and they were caught in my mess. I didn't give them the chance to have a normal family life. They already had absent fathers and now, my depression was making me absent. All they had were my parents and I became jealous as I wanted to be the mother they looked up to. I wanted to be the one they celebrated, but my depression left me in the background, and all of their memories were that I wasn't there for them because they were always at their grandparents'. My parents had taken over in their lives and I wanted them back. I thought that having solid relationships with men would give them the chance to feel normal, like their friends who had two-parent families, but they didn't understand why I wanted a man in my life. I wanted to protect them and I wanted our family's picture to look different, but while trying to create that picture, I created a bigger mess and they were left out as I focused on finding a man to help create that fake picture. The truth was that I was facing guilt. I wanted to take away the shame of single parenthood and the labels that went with my disrupted life, but it was too late; my depression had taken over. I was still broken inside as I had not dealt with the deep-rooted issues and I needed to fix my brokenness.

Chapter 11

Broken but Fixed

I was so damaged, and I wanted to be handled with care. When you buy goods online and your parcel is delivered, depending on the contents of the parcel, the parcel may say on the front, 'Handle with care', or 'Fragile, do not bend', and if the contents are damaged, it can be sent back to the distributor to be fixed, changed, or replaced. Who would handle this damaged parcel? Who would fix the pieces that were broken? Who would solve this? At that particular time, when I was questioned where I was, I could not see a way out. I had worn my mask for a long time, living a lie, pretending to be something I wasn't and believing my own lie. The truth of the matter, the answer to my question, was that I knew who the fixer to my problem was: our God, our Creator. He is the manufacturer of my life. He was the only one who knew the truth behind the mask, but how would I be fixed when I had walked away from God? For years, I lived in condemnation, brokenness and rejection. I needed to be fixed and have the pieces put back together again. Have you ever tried to put a jigsaw puzzle together and when you near the end, you realise that one of the pieces are missing and you become frustrated and annoyed, especially because you have come this far and you couldn't complete the puzzle? Nine times out of ten, would you just stop and dismantle the puzzle? The metaphor of not completing the puzzle is a sign of giving up and not being able to fix the problem, but what would it look like if you could find that missing piece and just complete that jigsaw puzzle? That was me. I was missing a piece — the end to my broken story — but I knew the story could not be completed or fixed without the author. The author was God. He knew the beginning to my end, so he knew which part of me needed fixing and He knew what He had designed for me. He had the template, the pattern, the person in me He had created earlier. I was created for a purpose. I knew I was being prepared with my pain, shame, guilt and mess, but being damaged gave me the revelation that my journey was taking me from pain to purpose. Every cycle of my life prepared me for a separate journey. Although I did not know it would come with pain, God knew what was in the parcel and He knew He had to carry that parcel with care, as the parcel had the words written on it: don't bend, it's fragile. The outside of the package looked good, but the inside was damaged. When the contents inside of a package are broken or destroyed, it has no value or worth until it is fixed or replaced. At times, I wanted to be replaced rather than fixed. I used to say, 'I wish I could go back to being 11 years old again. Like in the film 'Back to the Future', I wanted to go back to make changes and correct my faults and mistakes. I wanted another chance. I wanted to change my past of dropping out of school, being a teenage mother, being abused and failed relationships, but all of these failures and all of this pain helped produce my purpose to live, find my worth, value and place in society, to prove that my past failures, bad decision-making and wrong choices couldn't stop what once seemed impossible from becoming possible. We must trust the process of the new packaging and allow God to re-shape us, re-position us and fix those broken pieces. Then we must close all chapters of the past, accept our failures and accept that we were wrong because acceptance is closure. Try to forgive yourself and others and then you are ready to be delivered again. Closing the doors on old things gives you room to step into new things and start a new journey.

– Chapter 12 –

Silent Journeys

Through all of my life's journeys, I realised that I was silent. I had gone through a journey of silence. Silently, I had different life experiences that were not public, but my silence carried a secret shame and I had to fight that shame within. I had to either keep it in and allow the silence to kill me or speak and set myself free. My journeys have not been easy, but I am no longer silent, so here I share with you snippets of my thoughts on each of my silent journeys and how I closed each chapter, taking it from bitterness to a place of forgiveness.

Silent habits

Have you ever hidden your habits due to your job, family, religion, or position or status, you dealt with your issues silently? Well, I secretly hid my habits for years, keeping my habits silently inside of me. What was strange was that I heard so many people speak about these habits openly, but I found it too embarrassing because I was married. When I had broken up my previous marriage, I struggled with masturbation because I wasn't having regular sex with my ex-husband as he was seeing someone else. I often needed a release and this helped me to help myself. Some people would say it was natural to do so, but my religious beliefs sees masturbation as a sin, so I lived silently with this sin, living my life in condemnation. I realised that once you have had a sexual encounter and it suddenly stops, it becomes difficult to cut yourself off from that feeling. No one prepared me for separation or told me that I would struggle sexually, as one minute I was a married woman, making love with my husband and the next, I was a separated woman living in the same house but sleeping in separate rooms, wanting to make love to my husband, but I couldn't because we were separated. Due to my past feelings for him and how it made me feel, I had no self-control and I indulged in masturbation. Because I was still married in the eyes of others, I couldn't speak to anyone and I continued with my habit silently until I was divorced. I constantly abstained, repented, prayed and cried for forgiveness. Then, a couple of days later, the cycle began again and I was in a constant, messy cycle.

Silent depression

I never knew I was depressed, and I never knew that drinking alcohol was my cover up. Although I drank secretly due to a messed-up relationship, I didn't want anyone to know I was drinking, so I kept it hidden. I was seen as everyone's backbone, the leader, always in charge and everyone looked up to me. I had the answers and I knew how to help others. I knew what I wanted and where I wanted to go, but the truth was that alcohol was killing me inside and my future was dying. Dramatically, there was one incident that made me identify that the drinking needed to stop. I had a suspected heart attack. My drinking was getting out of hand and I was diminishing inside. I knew I had a choice. I would either become an alcoholic and die or live and save my family. In the end, I chose my family and health. The suspected heart attack was a wake-up call. I knew drink was no longer an option and I had to get myself together. I had to get out of that relationship to save myself and my family.

Silent rejection

Have you ever wanted something so badly, seen everyone else achieve what you want and all you can do is to smile, but you are secretly hurt that you weren't given the opportunity, even when you have the tools, experience and know how? Still, you were turned down, only to later find out the reason and it only confirmed your rejection. I applied for a certain position, and I was told I had not been there long enough to apply, but in a conversation one day, someone told me they had applied for the same role. They had been given the opportunity, although they had started at the same time as me. I was gutted at the silent rejection and I couldn't fight my case because the position was gone. Thoughts of the rejection played on my mind and I felt insecure about who I was. I thought that the other person was better than me and that I was not good enough. I had to watch her achieve that of which I was capable of doing too, and I was embarrassed inside and silently rejected.

Silent relationship

Have you ever met anyone who told you they liked you and they would love to be with you, but they didn't confirm their relationship status with you? Still, they made you feel like you were everything and no one else mattered but you and the words they spoke sounded honest, true and loving. They have a way of weaving you into their spell of love — or should I say lust — and the next minute, you're in their bed making out. After that moment of lust, you realise that there was no conversation about being in a relationship with them and you call a few days later and they don't answer, or the call goes to voicemail. Because you haven't discussed your relationship status, you can't ask why they aren't picking up or when you are going to see each other again because you're not their partner. You didn't have confirmation that you were an item at the beginning, so you have to forget they ever existed. You can't even complain to your friends or family about this silent partner, so you stay silently hurt, used and ashamed. All you can do is break up silently with people with whom you are not in a relationship with. My biggest silent embarrassment was when someone had fooled me into thinking they were a Christian, looking for a wife and would marry me the next day only to find out they had lured me into their bed and the marriage idea was fake and now I was silently dirty and living with condemnation. The fact is that public relationships make public announcements; silent relationships make hidden shame. If you can't announce me to the world, but you can sleep with me, then I am classified as a public, hidden shame. I heard someone say he had a woman for different times of the day. He said, 'Some women can only be seen at night with me as some are not good-looking enough to be seen in the day.'

Silent abuse

Have you ever been told by someone that if you had only done something, you would be in a different place, knowing that you are in that place because they put you there? Has anyone ever patronised you with 'woulda, coulda, shoulda', silently abusing you with words of hopelessness, brought up your past faults and used them against you, made statements like, 'Don't you think that you're the problem behind why all of your relationships ended?' made comments about how you look, built insecurities, made you feel like no one would ever want you because of how you looked or that you hadn't achieved anything yet? Even the look on their face speaks volumes and when they make a face of disgust about what you are wearing and how you look, it builds insecurities and diminishes your confidence, creating low-self-esteem. When you look in the mirror, all you can hear them say is, 'You're ugly. You're fat. You're worthless. You're too late. You will never become. You will never have. You're not worth anyone's time.' The more you hear these words, the deeper you go into your shell. Their words get louder and you prevent yourself from moving forward, believing the lies of your abuser.

Silent secrets

Have you ever made friends with someone of the opposite sex with whom you had no intentions of being other than friends, but silently, without them saying much, you sense they like you, but you ignore the signs and you say, 'I don't like them in that way'? However, silently, they have other plans for you. You invite a male friend over to help you to do something in your house and the evening turns

67

to sweet talk. Before you know it, your underwear is off and you're having sex. And to make matters worse, you're not in a relationship with him. The next day, you wake up with guilt, firstly because you're in a relationship with someone else and secondly, you're a devoted Christian. This becomes a silent secret. What hurts the most is when you see that person a couple of months later, he is hand in hand with his new fiancé, although you were in bed with him a couple of months ago. You can tell no one, but you have the feeling that you were not good enough to be married; you were only good enough for a one-night stand. Now you have to live with that for years and act like you're happy for the new couple when you are silently broken and ashamed.

Silent thoughts

Have you ever silently thought about where you would be if you had not experienced certain things or made certain decisions? Have you silently thought that you didn't want to be here any longer to face issues you created for yourself, silently angry with life, wishing you could end it in a moment, looking over the edge of a building and seeing yourself plastered on the floor, having a moment to think about what if you jumped? What would you leave behind if you have no dreams, no vision, no legacy and no hope for your family? When your eulogy is read, imagine the shame your family will have to face when people talk about you and how you took your life, the chit-chat behind closed doors. They were already talking about you when you were alive and the thought of being dead with your name living on, with their same abuse and hurt that you faced when you were alive.

MELISSA MARTIN

You can't win unless you make the change, so choose to live and start believing in yourself and stop the naysayers from talking. Begin to achieve and make a change.

Silent change

How can you change something that has already happened? How can you make changes when you have already been written off? Changes start from the heart. Out of your mouth, the abundance of your heart speaks. What is deeply rooted in your heart will speak one day and when your heart speaks, it will cause changes to your situation or circumstance. Have you ever had anyone tell you how you made them feel, but you weren't aware they had been carrying those feelings? When they confronted you, you were able to explain why and this gave them reassurance and you both had a better relationship after, but what happens when you know that some people haven't forgiven you and you can't make changes? Then, you're left with the guilt and they have stemmed un-forgiveness in their heart for you. They don't want to release you from the guilt, so they keep you there and you remain silently unchanged.

Silent un-forgiveness

Have you ever been so badly hurt that you don't want to release the person from their guilt, so you keep them there silently? There are no conversations, no answers, no confrontations, just total silence, although you know that, in your heart, they want to make peace and they would like the opportunity to argue their case, you silence their moment, but you feel they will only blame you for the incident. They don't want to take any responsibility, so you think that silence is the best treatment. This is true in some cases, but what might it feel like if you experienced physical pain and the pain was a metaphor for how it feels not to be forgiven? Once, I had pain in my body that was so bad I was admitted to the hospital. While I was there, the spirit of God revealed to me that my pain was like a lack of forgiveness. It was like if you arrived at the hospital and no one could locate where the pain came from or what the problem was. You waited for answers, but every test came back negative and the pain remained. Then, the last test which would have confirmed your illness came back inconclusive. How did it feel when you had no answers to the pain and you had to leave the hospital without answers, but the pain remained? This is the same as when you withhold your forgiveness from those who seek it, the daily pain they feel of not knowing or not being able to let things go. It's just like the test results where nothing was confirmed, but you could be living with an unknown illness and suddenly die. Catching the illness early could save you and give you a couple more years to live. It's just like un-forgiveness — that person will just die with guilt and you will carry your un-forgiveness until you die as nothing was never resolved. Releasing these feelings releases yourself so you can move on and live in perfect peace.

Silent hurt

What does silent hurt look like? A smile? A laugh? A hug? A conversation? Most often we don't recognise hurt as it is covered up by our normal activities and we wear masks of pride. We ask, 'Are you okay?' and answer, 'Yeah, I am fine. It's his loss. I am better off without him,' but we secretly hurt and our hurt turns to bitterness and we wish we were with him again, or even know why he left. Silently, you want him to see that you have changed — be it weight loss, a new car, a new look, a new partner, or a new job — you want him to see his loss and how great you have become. Although you want him to see that, you also want him to hurt like you, or you want the opportunity to get back with him, reverse the tables and hurt him too. This might satisfy your pride and stop the pain, but unfortunately, it will only make things worse. I went back several times to past relationships only to be hurt over and over again. Instead of resolving previous issues, you just add extra problems, and nothing is resolved.

Silent truth

When I was newly divorced and I wanted to start a new relationship, I knew that as a Christian, finding a new relationship wouldn't be easy. I had to have a solid foundation before marriage, but the silent truth was that I wanted a husband to satisfy my sexual needs rather than a desire to marry. At that time, I was only attracted people who wanted sex rather than men that were interested in marriage, but that is what I thought I also needed. I believed it would fill the gaps of healing after my divorce. I wasn't ready for marriage as I was still hurting, and I needed counsel and complete healing. There's a saying that you are attracted to who you are, so neither of the men I met at the time wanted marriage; they just wanted to have fun or pass the time. I went through a process of meeting different guys with different agendas, but my intentions were not right either. Although I loved the idea of marriage, the truth was that I was not ready.

Silent wait

How hard is it to wait, especially when you've been waiting for a long time? Everyone passes you by. They have already achieved that for which you have been waiting. It's embarrassing. Waiting is essential, as at the end of the wait, you will have the best. While waiting, I was preparing. I was being delivered from the norm. The guys who seemed nice had bad intentions. During the waiting process, God took me on a journey. I silently decided to give up my bad habits, struggles, fears and past hurt and embark on a journey of wait. I knew I hadn't been forgotten by God. I knew I was still in the race to achieve. I knew I had changed silently for my wait.

Chapter 13

The Assignment, The Snare and The Promise

Don't take 'finding' yourself a man or a woman for a relationship into your own hands. Pairing you with God's best is so much easier because God understands TIMING. It is dangerous to step out on your own time and date a bunch of random people that God never intended for you to see. Then, you experience all of this hurt, soul ties, drama, broken hearts and whatever else comes with it while God sits there saying, 'I had nothing to do with these men and women. I will restore you and make you whole, but you have to stop trying to control your life.' I know — right now, you're asking, 'How does God speak to you? How do you know who is best for you?' Well, some people call it fate, red flags, gut feelings, voices, or instinct, but I call it GOD — the one who speaks to me. Whomever speaks to you — a voice, instinct, or gut feeling — before we do things, we are all warned or have some type of feeling that something is not right about the person for whom we have looked. God has not forgotten about you, but you must ask if you forgot to trust Him on your journey. Trust is the biggest keyword in waiting and being guided on your journey to find love and you must trust that God has the best person in mind for you. Unfortunately, this wasn't the case for me. I trusted God to a certain point, but when the process became slow, I got older, or I saw everyone else getting married. I wanted to speed up the process and I started choosing random people and accepting any invitation to go out on dates. I finally got fed up waiting on the promise.

As Christians, we follow Christian principles and we believe that men should go out to look for their wives, and women should wait for them to find them. The famous Bible scripture, 'He that finds a wife finds a good thing,' this scripture had become a cliché for me. Having to wait for a man to find me took even longer, especially because I was a divorcee, a single parent and I was going through the healing process after being divorced. I decided that I wanted to help God on my journey to find love, dipping my fingers into the process. I wanted to take the driver's seat and let God hop into the backseat to support me when the journey got rough. Then, I would ask him to jump into the passenger's seat and when the steering wheel was unsteady, I would cry, 'HELP — take the wheel! Be the driver!' But, by that time, I had too many crashes, bumps and scratches that I could write off my car and start the journey of finding love all over again. The good thing is that it did not end in a fatal accident. I always recovered, but for some accidental relationships, I received compensation, though the person with whom I was involved said it was not his fault.

On the journey of finding love and waiting for my promise, I surrendered and gave God the driver's seat. I discovered that of those I had met along the way, some were my snares and some were my assignments and I would go down the road to meet my promise, only I followed God's instructions and let Him do all the navigating.

'God, take your place in my journey; take the wheel and let's go.'

Now let's look more closely at the assignment, the snare and the promise. What do I mean by these terms and how do they fit with my story?

For us to understand these three terms — assignment, snare and promise — we must first recognise into which category the people we meet fit.

The assignment

My understanding of these terms came when I met a person and the conversations turned to counselling sessions and I automatically built and encouraged him, so I knew he was an assignment. At the same time, my thoughts were that if I built him up, it would help him to be confident and he would be ready to be my husband. After the building process, he would know how to lead me, but the conversations usually end with, 'You will make a really good wife. Whoever you marry will be very happy.' Our conversations were never about me but always about him. It was then I realised that he was an assignment. This was so frustrating for me because when we first met, it felt like he could potentially fulfil my promise, only to find out he was just an assignment. The assignment was similar to the promise as he said the right things — that he wanted what I wanted — and he had good intentions and his vision was clear, but he was not in the right place, nor was he able to offer anything, as he was on his journey of becoming whole, learning his role as a husband, father and man. He was still dealing with a lack of forgiveness and hidden pain, so he had nothing to offer me in that process. Nevertheless, I wanted to fix him and make him mine because I am a fixer and a builder, but I wasn't on God's building site, as you can't create God's will for your life. It was frustrating as I wanted some of the people I dated to be my promise because their potential seemed great, but they weren't aligned with God's will for my life. Yet again, I was trying to do God's job because waiting took too long. I became an impatient and wanted it my way or the highway, so I started to meet the snares.

The snares

I identified this set of people by how they started their conversations and the way they spoke about their goals and dreams. They made me feel special and they said the right things. Some of them got right to the point and said they would love to marry me, often stating, 'I would marry you tomorrow.' To be honest, they were so good at their jobs of luring me into their deceit and lies. When I first met them, they sounded like the promise, with their promising words of marriage and how they would look after my family and me. Their visions and dreams were too good to be true, but I fell into their traps and the next thing I knew, I was giving them my life's savings or jumping into bed with them, or playing like they were my husband giving them husband benefits. They only saw me as 'friends with benefits', giving me lies on top of lies. I was so convinced they were honest. Although I saw the red flags and the signs — even my friends and family noticed they were snares — they convinced me to give them a chance and I lived in denial. Unfortunately, snares can't continue the lie for long because when they get what they want — be it money, sex, or your time — they are off. You know the saying, 'Why buy the cow when you can get the milk for free', in other words, why should they marry you when they can get the sex for free? At the end of it, your plans and goals are destroyed and all you are left with is shame, hurt and asking why me? Well, those whys are because you took on the journey of love by yourself, taking God out of the plans. If I had just waited, life would have been so much easier, but in the end, I decided to go on a journey of wait.

Before I started my journey of wait, I embarked on a journey of different experiences with different men. I went on a one-year journey and in that time, I had met six different guys. Can you believe it — not one of them was my promise? In my heart of hearts, I knew that one of them was my promise, but I also know that everyone is entitled to their own choice and everyone has the free will to choose, but to be honest, I wanted God to do the choosing. To make the journey easier, I wanted to give up my free will, so I decided to wait. Before I speak about my journey of wait, let me first tell you about my experience with the three men who were snares so you can understand how important it is for you to wait for your promise.

I met three men who were snares and three men who were assignments.

Snare Number 1: I met him on social media. I liked his picture. He commented and then he inboxed me and we started speaking. As he was the leader of his own church, he seemed responsible, focused and interesting. Our conversation went from texting to phone calls and we had the usual conversation about wanting to meet up. Because we discovered that we were both single and we both had the same vision, the encounter sounded like it was the promise. I was excited and I couldn't wait, but I was also taking things slow because I knew he was a highly respected person and he was a godly man. Still, something was niggling at me in the back of my mind that he was a leader without a wife, but I just shut out the what ifs. Believe me, those what ifs are so important to identify, but when we want something badly enough, we deny ourselves the truth.

One evening, I was out with friends and I had to stay at a hotel for the night due to the distance back to my house and my snare rang me. 'Where are you?' Wasn't it strange that the hotel at which I was staying was near where he was working that night? 'Let me come for you and let's go for a drive.' It seemed harmless.

Before you knew it, I was driving around London, he was holding my hand and it all felt romantic. Everything seemed perfect. It felt like he was the promise, with all the sweet nothings he whispered in my ears. However, his promises seemed too unreal, as it was our first meeting. Didn't I recognise anything strange? No, because he was telling me everything I wanted to hear, but that night went from holding hands to kissing and then his words of promise lured me back to my hotel room. 'Let's just have a coffee. Let's get to know each other a bit more.'

I trusted him and I trusted his religious leadership but was it the holding of his hands and the kissing that set me up for failure. Or maybe it was the invite for coffee, which went from having coffee to letting him have my milk for free and my thoughts about him being the promise went straight out of the window. Calls started going to voicemail and texts were blocked. A piece of me had been taken away. When I did get through to him, he used the pity party card: 'I was not in the right place. I just broke up with my fiancée and you came at the right time. I am sorry.'

Sorry, it was too late for me because I had to go back on my journey of wait, deliverance, healing and repentance. I had fallen for the snare, who I thought was the promise.

Snare Number 2: I met this person at work —how convenient. After meeting snare number 1, I thought I had learnt my lesson, but looking back, it was just a repeated cycle. Someone called me to say they were praying for me and they saw that I would marry an African man with an O in his surname. Because this person was a praying person, I believed him, and I took his word literally and started looking for African men. When I met African men, I asked them their surnames because I was believed that my promise was an African with the letter O in his surname. Well, strangely enough, the majority of men where I was working at the time were African and I am sure there were loads of men with O's in their surnames. Therefore I believed that all the men who took a liking to me were potential husbands and I tried to have an encounter with them in conversation, but I was also trying to do God's job again and I went looking, rather than waiting to be found.

Looking back today, I realise this was crazy — or should I say desperate — and I fell into the hands of snares. There was one guy I used to see in the reception area of my workplace. He would look at me inquisitively, but because he looked too young for me, I made no contact with him.

However, one day, while at work, he left the reception area to sit in my office and he started speaking to one of my colleagues about his cooking. My colleague was complimenting him on his great cooking and I jumped into the conversation, saying, 'Can you cook?' That was because a tick-box for my potential husband was that he had to know how to cook, so the cooking conversation drew me to him. Sometimes, we just need to keep our mouths closed and listen. The devil knows your desires, and he will use those desires to tempt you and take you away from your wait. Sometimes, when we become desperate, we choose anything and anyone, not realising that some people are counterfeits. They look and sound like the promise, but it sometimes so hard to identify which is real.

While he was in my office, our conversation moved away from cooking and we realised we had so much in common. When I looked at his name badge, his name started with the letter O! As our conversation continued, I sat at my desk, saying in my heart, 'Promise...Promise... This is the promise! Yes, God!' When I left to go home, he slipped his number to me and asked if he could attend my church with me. Not only was he an African man, but he also had an O in his surname and to top it all off, he had the same religious beliefs. Come on, God; this must be your promise.

We went on a first date and sat in the restaurant for over five hours talking and sharing. It was so natural and I had no reservations that this was not God at work. Finally, I felt as if I had met the other half of me. I even went to the extent to post online that I had been found by my Boaz — that's how serious it felt — but as time went on, I found out that he was just another snare who wanted money and sex and made me believe in his lies. First, he told me that he could not commit because though he was separated, he was still married, but he could not afford his divorce and he wanted me to help him. His story was so real and I trusted him because of his Christian faith, but he just was there to lure me into his bed, like a sheep in wolf's clothing. How could I still not know that he was a snare? Because he took longer to prey on me with sex, got me to trust him first, took me out on a couple of dates and made me dinner several times, so I felt respected and valued, but he was just waiting for the moment to capture me. After that moment, his conversation changed and he had no more time for me. All he had were excuses. Why? Again, because the milk was free.

Snare Number 3: Why do I always meet the same guys, fall into the same traps, have the same conversations and fall for the same promises, but I still can't identify that they are there for one thing and that one thing is not love and marriage? The very thing that we desire is the very thing at which we are tested. At that particular time in my journey, I so wanted to be married and I would do anything in my ability to achieve that. I hope you heard what I just said: 'in my ability.' That was my biggest problem — God was never a part of my choices and I never prayed about the men I met. It was so easy to allow myself to fall into the same cycle because God seemed like he was taking too long. I was getting older and my youngest daughter wanted that father figure and every night she prayed I would meet my husband, but I was running out of time. I needed my promise from God…NOW! So there I went again. I met another guy and I knew that he was not my promise. I knew he was a snare, but I was so fed up with waiting and all I wanted was to pass the time. I knew that I was going to a bad place, but I couldn't see how God was working as all the others were snares, so I decided to settle for a snare. This snare was, however, the worst. He told me that he was divorced and that he'd liked me for ages but couldn't approach me. This time, I could see that he was an outright player. He said the same things the last guy had said, but I wanted to see what would happen anyway. There was a part of me that wanted to believe he was truthful, but I knew that my life would get worse and that I might not recover from the consequences. It was a risk I, nevertheless, took.

It started with some FaceTime antics. Calling me late one night, he popped up on FaceTime fully naked. I was shocked, but it felt harmless. Though we were not having proper sex, he did masturbate. This went on for a while and it seemed safe but wrong. His FaceTime antics became real when we went on a long drive. It started off with just kissing until the windows became steamy and he was getting my milk for free in the back of the car. No one knew about it — just me and my snare — but it became difficult when I later found out that he was still married. Now, I was committing adultery and I hated myself for not waiting. I hated the lies. I hated that I had become desperate. I was in a bad place. I needed out and fast, so I pulled the pregnancy card as I knew he would run a mile. He knew it would break up his family, so he closed the connection. I haven't seen him since that day, but I've lived in guilt for ages because he was married, and I am so against cheating, but now, I was a cheater, too.

I needed to forgive him for his deceit and lies and I had to also forgive myself. It was much easier to deal with who were assignments because they didn't take a part of me away and they didn't expect anything but my time, encouragement and listening ear. At the end of our encounters, they left me with gratitude and hope, made me feel I was good enough to be married and encouraged me to wait. I knew that I was building them up for their own wives — to confirm this, they are all in relationships and waiting to be married or married already. My time with my 'assignments' ended, and they saw rewards after I'd built them up. At the time, I felt like meeting them had been a waste of time, but now I know it was necessary because if they had not been a part of my journey, I wouldn't have been able to identify these three types of people and I wouldn't have recognised my promise.

I had to go through the waiting stage again. Just like when you miss your turn on a motorway and you have to keep driving until you get to the next exit before starting your journey all over again and sometimes, the next exit is far away. This is like what happens when you don't do what you're supposed to do and you have to wait to start again. Sometimes, this means waiting for six months, a year, or maybe even five years. However, God is always on time and when you follow His way, you can't go wrong. All the mistakes indulging in the snares in my life could have been avoided if I had waited and listened. Listening and following instructions is something we don't like to do — how many times have you bought an item like a wardrobe from a hardware store and while you're in the middle of building it, you realise that it's the wrong way around and you pull it down and start to build it all over again? Why? Because we never follow the instructions in the box. You think that you have built that wardrobe many times, so it will be easy and you know what you are doing, but this is our biggest problem. We become complacent and think we are the same people after one month, six months, or even two years, but we change every day. What you could do two years ago — or even three weeks ago — you might not be able to do again due to your health, mood, people around you, or your environment, which can lead to mistakes.

How would I get to my promise if I kept disobeying and messing up? I didn't deserve God's promises — why would God give me my promise after I had secretly disgraced and betrayed our spiritual relationship? I felt like I wasn't worth being loved or worthy of being a wife. I felt so bad. There were so many women in my church that were waiting for their husbands and living a life of wholeness. They were waiting and obeying God, while I was not obeying and living in a mess, with the same expectation. But God is a forgiving God and He always had a plan for me. He already knew my mistakes and weaknesses; he was waiting for my full surrender and repenting heart. I was soon on a waiting journey. I had gone around the motorway several times, missed my exits and now I was on the straight and narrow road. God had taken His seat and He was now the driver and I was listening for His clear instructions like I would with a car navigator. Buckle up your seat belts and let me take you down the road with God on a journey of wait.

Chapter 14

Journey of Wait

The first instruction God gave my spirit was to buy my wedding dress. How bizarre when all I kept meeting were men who were snares or assignments and there were no signs of my promise. This was an act of faith, a God-given task, but to make the task harder, I was a student, and I had no job. How impossible it was — no man, no job, no money? Only God could come up with such an impossible idea, but it's written in the Bible that 'All things are possible with God.' I thought, well, if this is God, then open the doors of faith, I went wedding dress shopping. I consulted a faith-believing friend and told her what I had felt in my spirit and she said, 'Let's do this.'

My first appointment at the wedding dress shop was amazing. I tried on different dresses to find the best fit for my shape. 'This is it, fit and flare,' the shop assistant said, showing me this beautiful sparkling dress. When I left the fitting room with the dress God had in mind for me and my promise, tears rolled from my friend's eyes. 'Yes, this is it,' she said. When I looked in the mirror, I knew I had found my dress, but when I asked the price, my face changed from smiling to an expression that questioned how the right dress could be at such a wrong price.

The shop assistant said, 'Go on. This was made for. You can leave a deposit.' I had three months to pay it off and by my faith in God, I made my deposit and trusted God with the rest. God did the rest. I was blessed with money in my account and after the three-month period, I hung up my dress and waited for the next instructions. Every day I saw my dress, it was my reminder that I was getting married and that God had made me a promise. Although I had a promise, while waiting, all I met were snares. My dress hung there for ages. I was so frustrated with God. Imagine: no one knew I had my dress. Two years had passed by; I had no man and every day I looked at my dress, I was waiting for my promise with no idea of how or when it would happen. Can you see now why I took things into my own hands? I was frustrated and wasn't listening for further instructions and I gave up. Although I had messed up, I knew I was still on the journey towards my promise and I just had to get back to the original plan and wait and listen for instructions. It was then I heard, in my spirit, that I should 'get my house in order'. This was not my physical house but my body, mind and soul. I needed decluttering, re-shaping, healing, cleansing and cleaning because my spirit had also heard whilst at church; that by this time next year, I would be standing by my husband, so I knew I needed a quick detox in every area of my life; I needed to get my house in order.

I started with my home. I knew I had to create space for the man that was coming, so I had to clear out things I had been holding onto from my past: old pictures, phone numbers and clothes from my past relationships. I decluttered. I bought a new king-sized, ottoman style bed set and saved one side of the ottoman for my husband's clothes. I bought an extra chest of drawers, left it empty and cleared the rubbish from the bottom of the wardrobe to make space for his shoes. Next, I decorated: new floors, new walls and a large dining table around which I imagined we would have our family dinners together. I had to re-condition my single-minded self because I would soon be a wife with a family. I worked on each room individually, then I worked on the outside of the house, landscaped the driveway with stones and flowerpots. When this was done, I knew I had to work on my inner-self to build up my confidence after going through the experiences with the snares in my life. I disconnected from all who had caused me hurt or pain and I then detoxed from certain foods and fasted on several occasions with the focus of forgiving and letting things go. I gave away my car as I wanted to walk to work for fitness. Although I had struggled with my weight for years, at this point, I knew that I was enough and my new husband would love all of me, irrespective of my weight; however, I also knew that weight loss would increase my confidence and I wanted to look good for my dating season.

God had another plan. While waiting at the bus stop, I heard in my spirit, 'You're not at the bus stop because of your fitness. You're standing here because I am teaching you how to wait.'

'Whoa, God, this is getting serious,' I said, still waiting at the bus stop. It was then I understood that I was on a journey of wait. Still standing at the bus stop, God gave me a scenario of waiting and being on time. This is how I heard it: 'I am teaching you how to wait and I will get your promise to you on time.' When I heard that, I saw a bus at the end of the road. It went straight past the bus stop where I was waiting and this lady came out of nowhere and she said, 'When the bus is late, it won't stop here. It goes straight to the next stop.' Just then, I heard in my spirit, 'Just like that the bus that was late, the driver broke the rules to get his passengers to their destination on time, and that is what I will do for you. I will break all of the rules to get your promise to you on time.' That moment blew my mind and I knew that it was time to trust God's timing. I needed real faith and that required me to be totally focused. Sometimes, when God gives us a promise or an instruction, we want a step by step guide on what time and day God will fulfil that promise and when the guide is not straightforward, we doubt and ask the question, 'Is this is God or is it just my own thoughts?' but the quietness of God is sometimes a good thing. I heard a pastor say that when you are being directed by satellite navigation in your car, you hear the voice direct you when to turn or continue on, but when you are on a straight road and there are no turns, the voice is silent until the next instruction. This was such a powerful analogy. I had to trust God that his silence was good for me and I was on route to my promise. After following all of His instructions to get my house, mind and body in order, I was given the prophecy that my husband was at my church and I had to get ready.

'My church? That can't be true.' I was not convinced by this prophecy and my thoughts were, 'Here we go again,' as I had heard so many prophecies over the years that my husband was coming so I should get ready because my Boaz was on his way, so I thought they were just more dead words., however, there were times I thought this could be true because I was already on my journey of wait.

After this prophecy, I was constantly distracted. I met different guys from different races, cultures and colours and they showed me some interest, but unfortunately, none of them were from my church. There was one particular person who showed me some interest and yes, I nearly fell for his sweet words, forgetting that I was waiting on my promise at my church.

*****

One day, I was walking home from work, and this guy appeared from out of nowhere, almost running into me. I was startled. He was out of breath, saying that he was trying to keep fit. Then he said, 'How do you keep yourself looking so fine?' At that moment, I forgot the promise at my church, as there was a fine, tall, dark, handsome guy standing in front of me with his sweet words. His teeth were white and sparkling and his smile was gorgeous. He continued with his charm and then he said he had just given his life to Christ and just got a new job. He was pressing my buttons of love, I was ready to give him my number and then, out of nowhere, this drunk, red-faced, white man appeared. Have you ever watched YouTube and you're enjoying what you're watching and an advert pop up, interrupting,

91

and you have to wait for the advert to finish? Well, that's what it felt like at that moment. This man interrupted the sweet words from my tall, dark and handsome potential husband, with 'I keep telling him to wait. He just came out of prison and he needs to settle down first before trying to get a girlfriend. Well, if I saw you, I would chat you up, too.' I was in shock. It was then that I looked at the guy properly and I saw his dirty clothes and shoes and smelled alcohol on his breath. I was talking to a homeless person on the street who had just come out of prison. Don't get me wrong: I have no prejudices against anyone's mistakes, but he was in no place to be looking for me to be his wife. After his friend had ruined his character, he said, 'God bless you. Nice talking to you,' as I got on the bus and I heard in my spirit, 'That is your problem. You look at face value. You don't look deep into who you meet. You just go for a "type" and that type keeps getting you into trouble. I want you to start looking at their hearts and not just their outward appearances.'

The journey of waiting had just got harder, as now my choice of men was going to change because I had given up my free will and I wanted God's best choice. In my spirit I said to myself, 'You chose this time God. I am waiting on your promise.'

– Chapter 15 –

The Promise

Although I was waiting and I had a prophecy that my husband was from my church, God had to get my heart in the right place to receive him. I was so caught up in what my type was, what he did and the size of his bank account rather than the purpose of a husband and the role of a wife, because in my past, I had only experienced meeting people who led me to broken relationships, sex, lies and cheating. God wanted my attention. He wanted to soften my heart. He knew I had faced so much heartbreak and I had no trust in men, especially the men in the church, but God's plan was bigger than mine and I had to trust God that he would give me the best; God's best choice. He knew my perfect fit. He knew that the man who would come would be a reflection of me. Why would I want anything else? The question was, would God get it right? What an insult, but, yes, I am human. I had also made the choice for God to take away my free will so I would have nothing to do with the choosing and if it went wrong, this time it would all be on God.

I went away on holiday and while I was there, I attended a wedding and met some beautiful people, but to me, they were the strangest couples. When I looked at their outward appearances, I would never have put them together. They looked like mismatches to me. However, during my holiday, I spent time with two couples whom I branded the mismatched couples, but while I spent time with them, I observed the love they showed each other, which was mind-blowing. When I asked how long they'd been together, I thought they would say a couple of months or years, but to my surprise, they had been together for over ten years. It was then I realised that God was showing me how outward appearances weren't everything and you could love someone for their heart rather than just your type. The holiday was a divine setup and my heart went through a process and I clearly saw that love outweighs types.

Whoever God was giving me, He was re-conditioning my heart and mind to receive him. I struggled while writing this part of the chapter because although I believe today that I am married to my promise, there was another guy while I was waiting who I had my eyes on for a very long time. The strangest thing is that when I was given the prophecy that my husband was in my church, he also said there were two men, and he made the statement, 'He has been watching you for a long time, but he has found it difficult to approach you.'

Yeah — confusing.

I thought, 'WHY, God?' Now, I had to work out who it was. I had to make a choice. Do you understand why this part was so hard to write? It was because both men were promises from God, but I had to decide which one.

Let me begin with how this journey began with different men. Just to clarify, God is not an author of confusion, but when God presented both men to me, one had a beautiful heart and the other was financially stable and I heard in my spirit, 'What do you want — the heart or the money?' I replied, 'The heart,' and I was the one to make the decision to go with the one with the beautiful heart.

Promise One

A year after I was divorced, a man approached me to ask to be a part of the prayer team I headed in my church. That was my first contact with him. He seemed very excited, but he also seemed shy. I explained how to join and when he walked off, I said in my mind in a Jamaican accent, 'About you want to join the team, ah, woman, you ah look.' I knew from that very moment that he liked me, but I was not ready for marriage because I was still in the healing and forgiving stage of my life, so although there was an opportunity, I just wasn't ready. After that first encounter, we casually said hello while passing each other after church services. After the years of just saying hello, he became one of the brothers in the church, so I had no intention of making him my potential husband.

Promise Two

He was new to the church and when he arrived, he came with a female, so although my first impression was, 'Wow, who is that?' I knew he could potentially be that female's husband-to-be, so I didn't want to go there. Not long after, he was sitting alone, and she was nowhere to be found — was he single? I was not sure, but I was curious. To be honest, I fancied the man and I wished he had made some kind of contact with me, just even one time and I would have made him mine. Yeah, I know what you are thinking. Yes, I wanted to do God's job again, but I had to wait and that waiting happened over many years, but in the interim of waiting, I had dreams, visions about that guy. Because he never approached me, I thought he didn't like me, although in my heart, I knew he did. Years went by and he became another brother in the church.

One day, I went on holiday to New York for my birthday and at that point, I was so ready for marriage. While in New York, I went on a night bus tour. We went over the Brooklyn Bridge and the scenery and lights were beautiful. I imagined how nice it would be, sitting there, on the bus, holding hands with my future husband. So, I started to pray, giving God all the things I wanted in a man. I named everything I could possibly want and at the end of the prayer, promise number two came before me like a picture. It felt like God was saying that the man before me in my vision was everything for which I had just prayed. At the time, I didn't have the prophecy that my husband was in my church and the man had not made any moves, so, although spiritually, I believed he was a potential, I was still waiting on God. It was strange because I wanted him to speak to me, I would notice him speaking to everyone else, but I sensed a shyness when he saw me. It could also mean that he was not interested in me, so I had to let the idea go and I just decided to wait.

The Decision

I remember that it was Saturday evening and at that point, I had already had my prophecy that there were two men in my church who wanted to marry me. God had presented these two men before me and branded them as the one with the good heart and the one with the money, and I had to make a decision as to whom I wanted. Today, I realise that my decision to choose promise number one, the one with the good heart, was based on my past hurt and pain and I wanted a man with a good heart because I did not want to fall back into depression and I wanted to be happy. Some people would have gone for promise number two, the one with the money, especially after having all of the dreams and visions and because I had been so attracted to him from the first day I had seen him, but it was so important that, above the nice looks and money, the man I needed had to have a good heart. This time, I was not only going for face value; I wanted the heart.

That day, when I choose promise number one, God began to make it happen. The connection was surreal and there was no turning back. The timing was right and God was ready to give his promise to me, but at the back of my mind, I kept wondering if I had made the right choice. Can I be honest? Upon reflection, although I had told God I wanted the heart, the reason I didn't choose promise number two was that I thought I wasn't good enough for him. He seemed so well put together and financially stable and I had all my baggage, debts, and issues with my weight. I thought I was not his cup of tea. I had too many insecurities and it was easier to choose the one with the heart because I believed his heart would understand my past circumstances. I didn't want anyone asking why I hadn't arrived at a better place yet, so I decided choose the one with a good heart.

The next Sunday, I confirmed to choose the one with the good heart in my prayer. My first encounter with promise number one happened when I was coming out of church, walking with friends to my car and I looked behind me to see him walking behind me. 'Hi,' he said, kissing my forehead. The kiss was so memorable, intimate and new, as he had never greeted me in that way before. We chatted for a while as we walked to our cars. When I got to my car, the ladies with me couldn't stop laughing. I asked why they were laughing and one of them said, 'He proper loves you off. He didn't even see us and he didn't even greet us.' The other said, 'That could be her husband.' Even my friends had witnessed that our encounter was more than a casual hello. This led me to pray a little harder and trust God that He was going to do it.

The following week, while waiting for the church service to start, he came to sit next to me, between me and the same ladies who had laughed the week before, the ones who had noticed he'd liked me. He realised our seating arrangement was slightly cramped, so he decided to move behind me on another seat, but while he got up, he spilt my friend's water, and my friend requested that he get her a new cup of water. With no questions asked, he attended to the request. What he didn't know was that this humble heart gave him brownie points for it. After that night at church, I did not see him for around three weeks and I was worried if he would come back. At this point, I wanted to get to know him and hear his heart, but I felt as if it was on hold. What was God doing? What was the holdup? I started doubting, thinking he was another counterfeit. Was he not my promise?

One Saturday night, I broke down, crying in my room. While tears ran down my face, I prayed and it felt like I needed a release. The release of prayer was to let whatever was in the way of us having our encounter be broken. While I was praying, I could not see the man's face, but I could see his mouth, hands and feet and they were all chained up. I watched as the chains started to break, and when they had all broken, I felt a release. Then, I heard in my spirit, 'Not many days from now, I will manifest your husband and this time, no one can stop it.' Well, I had so many prophecies before and not see any sudden manifestations, so I was still apprehensive.

When I arrived at church the next day, I looked for promise number one and I could not see him. At that moment, I heard, 'Stop looking for him. He will find you,' so I focused on the speaker. That day, I remember the speaker saying, 'Do something different today. Confuse the devil and don't do what you would usually do,' so when church was over, I went straight home rather than saying hello to everyone — or should I say, looking for him? I went through the church doors and as I walked down the road towards the train station, I heard a beep from a car. When I looked over, it was Promise Number One, signalling for me to come over to the car and he offered me a lift. This was also new, as I had never been in his car and I was sitting in the car of the man I had not seen for the last three weeks. How had God pulled this one off?

'Where you going?' he asked.

'Oh, the train station,' I said, thinking it was too good to be true. Then, I took the liberty of repeating what the speaker had said. 'Well, you can do something different today and turn the car around and take me closer to my home.' It was done as soon as I had said it and he turned the car around so we were driving in the direction of my home. My promise from God was happening.

We started to talk, and he spoke of his testimony and what he had gone through and it was like looking in the mirror, as we almost had the same experiences. We had both been previously married for seven years, both partners had cheated, both had been engaged with the people in the church who had no intentions of marrying us for six years, both had dropped out of school, both of our daughters had been born on the same day and to top it all off, we were both prayer warriors. What more could I have wanted than someone who would understand my journey and who had an understanding heart? God made sure he'd had the same experiences as me so we would have the same vision of what we wanted in our futures. The journey of my promise had arrived. We both shared so much in the car we didn't realise that we were getting closer to my home, so he decided to take me all the way home. Outside of my house, he said, 'Before I go, let us pray.' Well, you know that he was going to get more brownie points.

'Wow, what a prayer,' I said before reminding him of when he had wanted to join my prayer team years ago. Before he left, we exchanged numbers and I knew God had things in hand.

A week later, we spoke every night for six weeks before agreeing to go on our first date. On the night of our date, we both knew we were leaving the friendship zone and going into the relationship zone; we were now dating. God's promise came true. Six months later, I was engaged and then, after nine months of dating, I was married to Promise Number One and God's word had come to pass: 'This time next year you will be standing by your husband.' I was happy and I had my promise.

Waiting and trusting God were the hardest parts of this situation, especially when I had been through broken relationships that had led me to depression and insecurity. As a result, I become more aware and are more cautious of choosing. However, I also know that sometimes, you can't choose the people to whom you are attracted, but unfortunately, they are normally the same people who will end up hurting you. So, giving up my free will and allowing God to choose was so much easier. Throughout the process, I encountered men who were snares and assignments, but God knew I was not ready for the promise and I had to go through my process from pain to promise.

Chapter 16

Forgiveness and Singleness

Although I had been given a promise from God and I knew he would follow through with it, I also knew I had to go through a process of being single and the process of forgiveness. I still had to forgive those who had hurt me before and after my divorce. After experiencing the snares and going through the rejection and the feeling of being used, it was so important that I went back to being a single person and had the time to reflect on what I wanted, rather than choose someone based on emotions and feelings or on a rebound. I needed to find myself and be single for real because all of the snares and assignments were relationships that were hidden relationships, and so, every time I had an encounter with these people, I was not preparing myself to be single. They were my security blankets. I wanted to be attached to someone as that was my way of not feeling lonely, but staying attached to them was not leaving room for my husband to find me. I kept meeting different men and after three months, I broke up with them. The more I entertained this behaviour, the longer it would take for my husband to arrive, so I had to ensure my singleness.

It was funny that when I was preparing to be single, I often saw a sign on the road that read 'single file traffic'. What stood out for me when I saw this sign was the word 'SINGLE'. I knew this was confirmation that I needed to be single, but how would I live a life of singleness when I hated being alone and I wanted to be married? You can't be married if you're not single first. It's a bit like not being able to walk before you crawl — there are steps to unions of marriage, as we all know that when you get married, two people become one, not two people become many. Those many other people are the ones we haven't forgiven or let go of, as they are still in our thoughts, in our phonebooks, in our photos in our phones, in our houses and in our conversations. Therefore, there is no room for the ones for whom we are waiting. We think it's okay to indulge in relationships or friendships while we wait for the right people, but our loneliness or impatience just brings delays, disruptions and confusion as we build things with people who will not be our life partners. You can become confused and even start believing he is the one, but you later then realise that you have wasted all that time.

One day, I had the revelation about singleness and that happiness is not found by finding a soulmate but by finding yourself, loving yourself and loving who you are. As you all know, I struggled with my past and I wanted to love myself first. I wanted to feel happy being single. I wanted to be comfortable living a life without the dates, texts and validations. Therefore, I had to go back to my first love, my first real relationship, the relationship without judgement, insecurity, or low self-esteem. I wanted God back in my life and I wanted to stop the pretense for my church brothers and sisters that I was serving

God. I wanted to stop engaging in a secret life of sin and this time, serve God for real. I wanted to put God first, but this can only be fulfilled through a real relationship with God. No one could love me better than Him. He knows every secret sin, every glaring fault and I had to learn how to forgive.

When I reflect on how much sin I committed during my walk with Christ and how God continuously forgave me each time, it was only right that I should forgive those who had done me wrong. It made me look at my Christian life from a different perspective — why should I be worthy of his promise, especially after all the things I had done? I wanted to let go of those past hurts, pain and bitterness. By living a life of purity and being devoted to God once again, He had brought me more joy than any physical or relationship pleasure ever could, so I was ready to forgive. I was ready to be single. I was ready to have closure.

Chapter 17

Closure

Acceptance is closure. Learning to accept that all that you have been through had been a part of your life's journey and understanding that every life experience has made you who you are today. When you accept your life's journey, whether good or bad, you can begin to close any open chapters. I call it 'just in case chapters' or 'what if chapters'. We sometimes say, 'What if he comes back into my life and he wants me back?' knowing full well that he destroyed you or used you, but sometimes, it so hard to close these chapters, especially when you don't know why it ended or why he treated you like he did. Sometimes, we wait for answers; what we are really doing is trying to keep the chapters open, but the risk of leaving some chapters open can destroy you later. I also understand that, on the other hand, we may say, 'Why should he get away with it? I need closure,' but unfortunately, not everyone wants to give you closure. In this case, you have to accept his behaviour, insults and abuse and just move on. Shrug your shoulders, shrug off the pain he has caused and erase his words from every chapter. Forgive yourself for not forgiving, then forgive him for REAL as this will actually facilitate your healing process. You can then begin to write a new chapter. What might that chapter look like? It will be written with words of love, joy, happiness and wholeness as you find your true you, building consistency, commitment, confidence, your worth, your ability to change, confidence and learning that you are more than your past. It sounds easy, but the process of going through a tunnel of pain and being able to flip the page to another chapter is not always straightforward and it takes persistence, being focused and determination, especially when you have to squeeze yourself through the tunnel to get to the other side to feel freedom. Many times, we get stuck halfway through the tunnel and we start reminiscing about the good days. We see friends who are connected to those open chapters. We see old photos and listen to old voicemails. We drive past restaurants we visited together and many more memories start flooding back. Moving on is at a standstill and closure becomes difficult. How did I come out on the other side of my tunnel? Firstly, I was stuck in my tunnel for years and I could not close the door or start a new chapter. Even when new chapters were open, the old chapters were always a part of my new beginning. I was stuck, not letting go, convincing myself there was hope, but first, let me speak about why it was hard to let go and why I kept the door open. I am sure you have heard the saying, 'you will never love anyone like your first love.' Well, that was me and in spite of the breakup, family dynamics and the hurt that it caused. I still held on and could not physically close that chapter. It took 15 years for me to first close the door — yes, I said 15 years to close the chapter for the first time. Then, foolishly, while stuck in the tunnel, I re-opened the door after three years of it being closed, and opening that chapter was a disaster.

When we first met, he was the love of my life. I felt like I was experiencing true love. I was so happy and I constantly had a smile on my face. Even my friends and family saw my change. Finally, I had a chance to be happy.

But what happens when your family is not happy with your choice? Togetherness cannot be fulfilled and the opinions of others only bring division and separation. What if you believe this person is your promise, but you feel opposed to the relationship and you have to leave behind the very person who made you happy? How can you comprehend it when happiness turns into depression? Yes, this breakup was serious enough to cause depression. First, I thought he was my promise. Second, I was happy, confident, I had self-worth, felt respected, felt loved and he was everything I wanted in a man and even more. Now, I was faced with a traumatic breakup and living with depression. I had lost all confidence, became lonely, self-isolated, started overeating and became angry. I blamed those who were against our relationship. I wouldn't go out, dress up, or even call my friends and family because I was no longer happy and my smile had turned into tears. I cried myself to sleep at night after binge eating and I could not see a future with anyone but him. I was stuck and I could not accept it was over. Even when meeting other guys, he was in my opening speech. They had to know about him and how he had treated me as I wanted to use him as a template, but I was just comparing him to them and no one could come close.

I would look for guys who looked similar to him, hoping they had his way of thinking, but each time I was disappointed and it led to a breakup. I was stuck in my past and I didn't know how to get out of it. I thought that marrying someone else would help, but in fact, it made it worse because he was constantly on my mind, when I got married the first time. I kept saying that I had made the wrong choice and I should have waited because he would have married me. I destroyed my first marriage. I was not free. All I did was compare. Although it was not a good marriage for other reasons, in my mind, I was still deliberating over whether he was God's perfect choice and I ruined it.

After my divorce, I took the opportunity to reconnect with him, only to find out that he had not forgiven me for marrying another guy, but that was just his excuse — was he ever going to marry me? Looking back on it today, I would say he was not because I believe that nothing or no one can stop two people who say they love each other from being joined. I think there were other agendas and I was played for a fool for years financially, mentally and emotionally. The love I had turned into dislike after our first reconnection. There was no respect from him. He put me down. He elevated my insecurities. He spoke of what-ifs and made me feel guilty for marrying someone else, but he confirmed that I was not a consideration in his life, and he was certainly not going to marry me. Strangely, I still had hope. I stayed stuck in that tunnel, waiting for the day he would change his mind.

Three years later, I saw some old pictures. Friends questioned why I hadn't met anyone serious. They wondered if he had been my promise. I was still stuck, reminiscing on the days we shared. As I spoke of in the previous chapter, I was just meeting snares and assignments. I also blamed myself that I was meeting the snares because I missed marrying this person whom I loved. All of these thoughts all came to an end when we reconnected again. Reconnecting resurfaced the past and he decided to give me a piece of his mind and he told me that he never wanted anything to do with me again. The word 'again' was my full stop. I saw it in capital letters in front of me. His AGAIN was my END. I was in denial for years and I knew I just needed an extra push to get through to the end of the tunnel. I had to take control of my feelings and emotions. I knew there was going to be freedom on the other side of the tunnel and I was getting out. I had finally made the decision to leave. I had wasted so many years wanting something that was never going to happen and I was forced to stay in that place for so many years because he never told me that he couldn't forgive me until seven years later. I had been stuck in hope, believing there was a chance, but that was his way of controlling me from afar, as he often said, 'I would marry you tomorrow,' but that was his way of holding me where he wanted me — my punishment of a lack of forgiveness. He knew I had loved him, and I wanted him and him only. Although over the years I had met other guys, he knew I would always come back to him and he was so right.

After the last encounter with him, I didn't want another relationship because I had turned bitter towards men, especially the men at church. I remember telling a friend that I didn't want a man from the church, that they were worse than the men outside of the church. I was so angry, and I was building up my pride and un-forgiveness, but my friend reminded me that there was a promise for me, and I should accept, forgive and repent. This made me realise that acceptance is closure. Now, I could embark on my new chapter, only this time, I knew who the author was, and it was God.

Chapter 18

Letting It All Go

I was so bitter over the years. After facing a broken engagement, divorce, miscarriage, rejection and indulging in masturbation and fornication, letting go was one of the hardest things. The worst thing about it was that it was in church. I suppose you're all saying, 'In church — how?' I was ashamed that I wore a mask while praising God. I messed up. No-one is to be blamed for my actions but me, but I blame my past. I needed to be set free. I had reverted to my old ways and I had brought them into the church. Don't get me wrong — although I struggled, I still had a relationship with God. I was still doing the work of God and I didn't allow my battles and struggles to stop me. Every time I sinned, I went to read Psalm 51 and repented. I know many Christians who have fallen off the wagon who can relate to Psalm 51's cycle of repentance after fornication, masturbation, or lying. There was a constant battle in my mind while I was being used by God and doing the work of God in church and struggling with my past sexual habits.

I would set myself up for failure each time. Why go to a place that could lead you to fornication or a space where you're hidden? When we say, 'I never knew that was going to happen,' it's a lie. We had an idea, but we just hoped it wouldn't happen. Unfortunately, we wrestle with our flesh, often putting the spirit of God on the shelf. I know that most believers in God often struggle with something; no one is perfect and it's a hard road to stay focused without some drama. If you're not tested sexually, it may be practically, spiritually, or financially, but there always something.

Anyone can struggle, no matter which faith, religion, or race to which you belong. One day, I was invited to a three-day church conference. I couldn't attend all three days, but the day I decided to go, I got a notification when I arrived at the building that it was cancelled. When I was there, I asked a young man who was passing by if I was in the right place and he replied 'yes', but then he commented on how I looked: 'You look nice — where you going?' to which I replied, 'Church.' When I realised it had been cancelled, I sat in my car and meditated on why I had gone there and why was it cancelled and surprisingly, the same young man who had given me directions knocked on my car window and said, 'You're so beautiful — could I get your number?' Now, I want you to picture this: he was a good-looking, young, Indian man who looked ten years younger than me. Straightaway, I thought he was Muslim due to his outfit. My response was, 'I am married,' which I wasn't at the time, but I was in shock. At that point in my life, I wasn't struggling sexually, and I was in a good place, sincerely waiting for my husband. Although I knew the guy wasn't my husband, I was curious as to why he had chosen me and I suspected he might be an assignment.

I called him back to my car — now, he was a stranger and it was night-time and he could have been anyone — and I allowed him to sit in my car to explore why he had wanted my number. I was correct that he was Muslim and he was about to get married. He explained that he was struggling while waiting to get married and he needed sex. His intention was for us to go to have sex in a hotel room if I had agreed to give him my number. Although he was getting married in three months, when he explained his intentions, I told him straight that he was not ready for marriage and if I had agreed to give him my number and go to a hotel, he would have destroyed his engagement for just five minutes of sexual pleasure. I spoke words of wisdom to encourage him that what he was doing was wrong and that he was already jeopardising his relationship for a one-night stand, which could lead to many more one-night stands, especially if he gets away with it.

He cried — he was so ashamed of his actions — but I understood his struggle because that was me once — or should I say that was me many times before. I realised that the struggle is real and when you start a habit, it is sometimes hard to break.

My biggest struggle was masturbation. After giving my life to God, I fornicated and when the fornication was over, I needed a fix. I thought that I was not harming anyone because I was the only one who knew, but I was destroying my relationship with God as I was becoming hooked. I turned to porn as masturbation got boring without watching porn. I was in a right mess. I remember when God warned me about stopping, but I continued. One morning, before dropping my daughter off to school, I indulged in masturbation. When we arrived at the school and we parked the car, my daughter slammed her finger in the car door and she had to be rushed to A&E. She left the hospital with two stitches; God had reminded me of my sin. In my spirit, I heard the scripture from the Bible: 'the sins of the mother and father fall upon the children,' and I realised that the same fingers she had slammed in the car door were the same fingers I used to masturbate. At that moment, I had the fear of God. It brought me back to something that someone had said one day, that if I continued to masturbate, I would not be satisfied with penetration when my husband came and would only want to use my fingers. I didn't want that for my husband. I wanted to stop. I wanted to let go of my habit. I wanted to start my walk with God. The devil knew my weakness; I was often tested and most times I failed, but before I could start over, I had to let go of all the mistakes, self-blame, fornication, masturbation, rejection and promises from those who had stolen my dignity and my body parts. I wanted my body back, only this time, for real. I was giving my body back to God. I wanted my temple to be ready for the husband God was giving me and I made up in my mind that I would not have sex with my husband-to-be before marriage. I had to let go of every soul tie connected to me. I had to forgive myself and those who had taken what was not theirs, especially those who had lied to me that they were single when they were still married, those who promised to marry me but who just wanted sex or money.

It was so hard, but it was a process and it took fasting, praying, deliverance and healing, but I knew that, at the end of the process, God had something better for me and I deserved to be loved, that I was valuable and worth the wait. When I did meet my husband, we both agreed that we would wait until we were married before having sex and for the first time in a relationship, it wasn't about sex and I felt honoured, respected, worthy, clean and loved. I was delivered from my habits and I was starting my journey of purity.

Chapter 19

Re-introducing Myself

How do you re-introduce yourself when all of your life, the people around you have only seen you one way although throughout your years you have done so much and had so many achievements? You've had some good days and some bad days, but they still just see what they want to see. Isn't it strange when you haven't seen someone for years, such as your old school friends and you say, 'I have four children, five grandchildren, I'm married, I'm a nurse and I inspire and mentor young women with children around the world,' and all they remember about you was as the class clown who dropped out of school and became a teenage mother? Does it sit right with the one who is listening? I didn't think so. If it were me, I would say, 'Who are you talking about? That's not the Melissa I knew,' but yes, that was me. I had achieved, I had changed and I was now ready to re-introduce myself to my naysayers, my dream blockers and those who believed that all I was good for was having babies and receiving income support benefits. They couldn't see my true ambition hidden inside of me.

I had to know who I was before I could become someone, so I had to go back to the beginning. My beginning was when my mum had asked me, 'What do you want to be when you grow up?' My reply was, 'A nurse.' That was my dream and my passion, but how would I get there with three children, my brokenness, my hurt, my shame and no qualifications?

Take One — Knowing Who I Was

Who am I? That was the question I asked myself. I wanted another chance so I could be someone rather than just a string of labels that formed who I would become. I needed an opportunity of hope. I needed change and the only person stopping me was myself. My second chance started when I became a Christian. The old me was going and I was forming into a new person. I began seeing my worth and my ability to be better. Attending church services week after week filled me with inspiration and I wanted more. The speaker at one of the services said to me, 'It's not too late to go back to school.' Those words of encouragement resided in my heart and I wanted to know how I would make this possible. Yes, the doubt and the words 'It's too late' rang in my ears. How could I go to university to achieve this without a current education? I wasn't even sure if I was an academic, but I knew I had God by my side and that was my motivation. I decided to apply for Bible school at my church. I wanted a challenge and that was my biggest challenge as it was at the university level and I hadn't even gone to college, let alone university. On my first assignment at Bible school, I achieved a C.

On the next one, I got a B. Then, after that, I got straight A's. I even achieved an A+. I was on the road to winning and finding out who I was. Everything that had been said about me by my teachers in school were evidently not true statements of my ability, and I was more than those labels. They had told me, 'You will not amount to anything. You will never be anyone. You won't get a job. No one will hire you,' but I was discovering myself; I had found a new Melissa. I was able to read, write, concentrate, be focused and I was more determined. I gave myself time to think about what had been lost and how I acted at school. While thinking about these things, I also found ways to do things differently the next time.

One evening, I was on my way to church and I took a taxi and the driver encouraged me. I found it really strange as he was a taxi driver, but he said, 'If you don't remember anything else from our conversation, I want you to remember three things: always have a relationship with God; get a profession; and have a good marriage.' After hearing this, I was inspired. Out of these three things, what stood out most to me was to go and get a profession. It was then that my passion to become a nurse came to life and I prayed to God to lead me to the right people. That week, I was travelling on the bus to my friend's house and I met an old friend I hadn't seen for years. We were catching up when she said she was on her way to a biology lesson. 'Huh. Biology,' I replied, as this person was older than me. She explained that she was a student midwife and she told me how she got into the course. I couldn't believe there was a course at college for mature students that could lead to university where you could become a nurse. The next day, I signed up for the course. Weeks later, I took an assessment; I was on my journey to life as a student and it was time to believe in myself.

Take Two — Transition

Believing in who I am was the hardest part for me, as I never believed. I was no more than a single mother, someone with dead-end jobs because I had no qualifications, but now, I was going to have the title of being a nurse. I was becoming the person I was told I never would be. I was transitioning into someone with a good title that was respected by society. I battled with this transition for a long time, as in the middle of transitioning, I had moments of disturbance that caused me to talk myself out of completing the degree in the normal three-year completion time. It took me 12 years to complete my studies as they were interrupted three times due to family disruptions, divorce and moving house. During these traumatic, stressful situations, I gave up the fight to become and began thinking that I didn't deserve to be better and this was going to be my life.

The first interruption came in my final year and I had five years to go back and complete, but the year I was supposed to go back, I was pregnant. You can imagine my thoughts. Those labels came back: 'You're just someone who has babies.' My career was on hold, not because I couldn't do it, but because I had given up believing, so I had written myself off and concentrated on being a mother. Although I regretted giving up, there was still a part of me that fought for my success, so I started working in the hospital as a health care assistant.

I remember the feeling of starting a new job and putting on a nurse's tunic and I knew I was still on the road to becoming a nurse. I went on to work with mental health patients, and it was there that one of my patients asked, 'Why don't you go back to university to become a mental health nurse as you're doing it now?' I realised that the patient was right. It wasn't too late to pursue my career as a nurse. I also remembered the preacher's words: 'It's not too late to go back to school.' It was time to push away the outside chaos and the shame of being in my final year at university and having to start again by going back to college as my first qualifications were outdated. I was determined that this was my childhood passion and I wanted to do it for my children. Although they saw me struggle and I wasn't the best mum, I wanted them to know that even if they experienced bad situations and some delays, they would remember my fight be inspired to never give up on their dreams and fight for what they want.

After all of the interruptions and fights, I was in my final year and the battle to complete it felt like it had just started. I had opposition from my course tutor and my placement manager. I had only failed one of my exams throughout my entire course and the re-take would determine whether I would take my crown as a 12-year survivor or I would go back to feeling like a failure. Have you ever watched the singing program 'The Voice'? Just before the singers are about to compete with each other, they say, 'Let the battles begin.' This was me — my battle to complete my course had just started.

The last three months of completing my course were like hell. I had panic attacks, I was stressed, my depression came back and it was trying to take me over. I just couldn't see the finishing line. After all of the stopping and starting throughout, I was still fighting to complete my degree at the very end with those who held my grades and performance in their hands. The first obstacle was with my mentor. She had the final say in my performance and whether I was competent to become a nurse and she knew she had the power to stop me. When we first met, I explained that I had previously studied, and I had numerous health care experience. To be honest, I was almost more qualified than her, but without the paperwork to prove it and my experience intimidated her, she was going to make sure that she would ruin my journey. At the time, all students were guaranteed a job at the end, without an interview. All we had to do was express the area of nursing in which we would like to start. I wanted community and young women and children. I was given a job to work in the community for a few days and then a few days on the ward with mothers and babies. It was my dream role, but my mentor decided to give me a bad reference and I was turned down. Now, I had no job waiting for me after qualifying. She was the same person who would sign me off to say that I was a competent nurse. My career was on the line and I had to get the director of nursing involved, as I had not gone that far to allow some random person to stop my progress. When the director of nursing read the comments, she had made in my performance book it did not correspond with my reference. I cried when I read that reference. How could someone that had given me such lovely feedback in my performance book say such degrading and belittling comments? Because she was a manager, she also had the power to get my tutor to back her up, but God was my source; He had the final say. The nursing director was appalled and called me to ensure me that when I qualified, a job would be waiting for me, but the job I wanted was already gone. Therefore, I had to leave my comfort zone and apply for the job I wanted and not the one I would have been given. At that point, I had no confidence in myself or my performance as I still had insecurities, especially when taking tests and the new job required me to take a day assessment, which included showing my confidence and skill. When you are backed into a corner, it gives you a different type of confidence, one that says, 'I am going to prove to my naysayers that I can do this.' At the end of the assessment, not only was I given a job — I was given two jobs, giving me a choice. I had two managers interviewing me for two different jobs and they competed in the interview to convince me why I should take the position with them. My confidence went from zero to 100. I had nearly given up and relinquished my right to be better, but there was one last hurdle to jump over and that the re-take of my assignment. Can you believe that my tutor told me the reason I failed was to teach me a lesson so I would push harder the next time? How could that be a valid reason to fail me? You must know that this was no ordinary nursing course and it needed a true fighter to survive to the end. Just before the results, I went on my knees to pray, and in my spirit, I heard, 'He wanted to fail you, but I turned his hand.' When I got up from praying, an email notification came through and I panicked, but I trusted God at the same time. As I opened the email, I screamed because now it made sense that

I heard. 'He was going to fail you' when I prayed, because my results were 41 and the pass mark is 40. Well, my journey of survival ended and I transitioned from a student nurse into a nurse.

Take Three — Letting Everyone Know Who I Am

How lovely was the feeling that, when asked, 'What do you do?' I could say that I was a nurse? How people's faces changed from curiosity to surprise, but they didn't know my story. All they saw was the end product and they were either happy or curious as to how I got there, especially because my past was not my future. I wanted to tell the world that I had achieved my goal, that I had survived through depression, being cheated on, divorce, moved out of marital home, suicidal thoughts and rejection. My journey had been so lonely that I couldn't tell anyone I found things hard because all I wanted was to give my children an inspirational story. If I had told them that I wasn't coping at the time, it could end up being my excuse to give up. Instead, I ensured that everyone would know I was a fighter and I had been given a second chance to become me and not my stereotype. I also reminded others that whether you are married, single, divorced, or mentally unwell, you can still achieve. It was time to let everyone know who I was, so I decided to inspire young people about my past and how I achieved a different path after years of perseverance, even having faced depression, rejection and lack of confidence. I wanted to show that these were not my weakness but a part of my strength. I also realise that when you don't know who you are or your worth and you lack confidence, it sometimes gives your competitors the chance to use your weakness to place you into a box, shut the lid and nail it closed. They only open it when you show your weak side so they can use their strength of confidence to outshine you. If you show any strength or confidence, they criticise you, give someone else the credit, or will challenge you, knowing full well your weaknesses. Then, they put you right back into your box of weakness. Showing more confidence could go against you but showing no confidence can pose a problem that you can't solve. My suggestion is to remember who you are and your capabilities, skills and passion and this will drive you to persevere, even when delays, obstacles and criticism comes your way. Be a true survivor so you can be the best version of yourself.

From the darkness of depression to a light of purpose and fulfilment.

Chapter 20

How to be the Best Version of Yourself

What does the best version of you look like? It looks how you envision it. I could see myself walking through the hospital in my nurse's tunic, injecting patients, giving medication, speaking to families, attending medical team meetings, having a nice big house, a nice car, a retreat home for young depressed mothers, a great husband, travelling around the world, and telling my story of hope. This was what I saw. This was the better version of me, but I was depressed, had low self-esteem, I was tired and lonely with no confidence and I had no motivation to become until the day I fought to be a nurse. I was told that I was more than a nurse and my expectations of who I was became clear. I could now see my patients, my retreat building, my husband, my house and I being my own boss. I was the owner of my own ideas and I needed to make that a reality by saying, 'Hello, my name is Melissa — what can I do to help?' I was now helping others to become what they saw themselves has. I had to examine each area of my life in detail, but before setting my goals, I had to consider my starting point, measure my progress and compare myself only with myself — or my previous self, to be exact. What is important is that you compete with your past status first. You must start thinking about how to achieve the best for you. Your mind is your greatest asset to nurture, create and deliver as much value as possible. You should also take care of your mind and make good life decisions, but we know that life's experiences can distort our decisions; but we also know that they are temporary. Although I was not focused on when I would complete my goals, I knew I was determined to jump over every wall and leap over every pothole to arrive and I focused on the finish line rather than the timescale to get there. When you compete in a race such as the London Marathon, some people don't watch the time they take to get to the finishing line — they just want to know that they completed the race so they can say, 'I ran in the marathon race, I know that I didn't win, but I am a winner because I made it to the end of the marathon.'

I ran the race of achieving for several years, but I knew there would come a day when I would see the white tape on the ground and I would run over it with cameras flashing, hands clapping and someone patting my back saying, 'Well done.' I knew that, after the race, I would exceed my hopes and dreams and I would live my best life. I was now a wife, business owner, nurse, counsellor, mentor and now an author.

How did I build my confidence? After having experienced so many setbacks, I was determined to help young mothers fulfil their purpose and I knew that if they heard my story, they would have some hope. I had to get my mind in the right place. I knew there were people waiting for this book and I couldn't allow my vision to die, so I had to explore seven different areas in my life: my mind, my body, my emotions, my spirit, my relationships, my assets and my career. These were the areas that I had to improve to become the best version of my ideal self. These seven areas would make up the whole me, the whole person. They work hand in hand and if one area is not completed, you can't achieve the best you. I didn't want to go back to the old me. I never wanted to look back. I was on the road to being the best version of myself!

Chapter 21

Never Look Back

Looking back wasn't an option for me. I made up my mind that, despite my circumstances and past issues, this time I was moving forward and I aspired to greatness. No longer would I allow my weight, status, or past to stop me. For the first time, I was ready to face my audience. I was ready to tell my story. I was no longer intimated or ashamed. My mirror reflected another person and that person was me. In the mirror, she looked strong, beautiful, confident, happy and grateful and she made me believe that I would not go back to that other person. She was dead, the new me had come to life and there was no stopping me. I had a voice and a survival story and there were women and men who needed a survival pack to continue and I would shout it from the rooftops that you can beat addiction, abuse, guilt, shame, rejection and a lack of forgiveness. There is still hope for everyone. Looking back was not an option for me as looking back would just show me the same old reflection.

Changing my name

I decided to change my name back in 2016. Yes, literally — I changed my name by deed poll to 'Christian-Milan'. I needed a new introduction, so I needed a new me. I wanted to erase the old me and I felt like using a completely new name would give me a fresh start. I didn't like the baggage that came with my old name. Melissa was abused, deceitful, hurt, depressed, damaged, unclean and ashamed, but I wanted to give her another chance. It was bizarre because when I looked at some Bible stories — such as the women at the well, the woman with the issue of blood, the man that was blind at birth and the man sitting at the pool — none of these people have names. Rather, they are all known by their experiences, but their experiences changed their names. Each story has a positive outcome. Consider the women at the well. At the end of her story, she was no longer called the woman at the well because she had an encounter with Jesus, he took away her past shame of having many husbands and she experienced God's salvation. Now, she was named the evangelist. Because I wanted my experience to have a positive outcome, I changed my name. At first, it felt amazing, almost as if I had been born all over again but without the experience of my mother giving birth to me. Sadly, it felt like Melissa had died.

Christian-Milan had a different start. She had new ideas, her mode of thinking had changed, her old ways had died and she had plans. She was making things happen, starting her business, writing up business plans and creating her website, business cards and leaflets. She even started organising events to share her story, but her story was Melissa's story, so the name change was just a coverup, masking

Melissa. I was angry with Melissa and I wanted her to disappear. I was still bitter about my past experiences filled with pain and unforgiveness. I knew my name change wasn't going to free me. It was my heart that I needed to get right to give Melissa the chance to live again and remind her that it wasn't all her fault. She was loved, beautiful, courageous, amazing and now she was inspiring. I decided to start over and I changed my name back to Melissa. Melissa — no introductions needed!

Chapter 22

No Introduction is Needed

Have you ever watched a movie and at the end you say, 'That was so rubbish — how could it end like that?' Well, those were my thoughts at the end of my chapter on depression. I knew people would no longer tell me that I never turn up or I never returned calls because I had finally found me. I was no longer living a lie and I was a new Melissa. I now knew that I wanted the story of my life to end differently. I wanted people to say 'wow' when they heard my story, saw my movie and/or knew my experience. I wanted my story to end with a great line. I wanted the world to read my story and hear my voice. I wanted to reach out to millions of women and men, not for fame or money but to let everyone know that you have power to change your story, whether at the start, middle, or end of your journey of life. I can give many testimonies/ that it can be done. I no longer need to introduce myself as a nurse as I have improved my expectations and I now carry many titles. I no longer have to live behind the title of being a nurse to prove that I am someone because my actions at work made me more than just a title. My life experience and the power behind my story was my strength, so instead of looking for someone to validate that I had finally become someone, my story spoke for itself. I remember seeing a family member that I had not seen for ages. When she saw me, she said, 'Wow! You look different. What has changed? What do you do?' When I told her my many titles, she replied, 'I can see you've changed.' It was then that I knew I didn't need any introductions. You can look, sound and walk like your purpose and those who don't believe in your change will see the end results. True achievers don't walk around telling everyone their achievements — those are the ones seeking validation as being validated confirms to us that our labels and stereotypes have changed. I had to get to a place where my title as a nurse did not make me who I was — it was just my first achievement as I progressed to go on to do better things. I was going to use these new skills to aim for new aspirations. I was no longer limited to one achievement or looking for validation. When you have gone through so much on your life's journey, it sometimes forces you to become strong-minded and when someone says something negative, you're reminded of the strength you have. That way, when you hear negativity, all you do is laugh and, in your heart, you say, 'If only you knew what I have been through; your negative words mean nothing to me.' I had finally overcome my battles and I was now on the road to being a work in progress as being the new me would always require constant evolution.

The Rest is Still Unwritten

Unfortunately, time is of the essence and everything cannot be written down here, but this allows us room to continue the story. When there are still things untold, you might question, 'What is next?' Well, for me, there will be more life experiences to come; therefore, there will be more inspirational stories to tell.

About the Author

Melissa is a mother of four, a wife, a counsellor, a mentor, inspirational speaker and founder of 'The Well Experience Project.' The project's aim is to help people who've experienced trauma through coaching, motivating, mentoring and empowering them back to a life of hope.

Melissa's life has not been an open book, and for most of her life, she wore a mask and hid behind her shame and pain. Inspired by her reflections of the Bible verse 'The woman at the well' (John 4), she knew one day she would need to remove her own mask and unveil the truth of her abuse, hurt, pain, shame and rejection.

Tired of a life filled with trauma, setbacks and depression, she decided to create new chapters in her life. After dropping out of school and being a single parent, she fought her way through, completed a bachelor's honours degree as a psychiatric nurse, went further to complete her master's in Health and Social Care and also gained a Highest Achievers Award.

Melissa aims to continue to inspire people all over the world and support others through their life journey so that they stay on the right path, re-focus, fulfil their dreams, careers and visions.

Acknowledgments

This book could never have been completed without the support and encouragement from those who cheered me on and sent words of inspiration, telling me my book would be sold to millions around the world and I would become a world-class author. These words kept me up and busy most nights, weekends and in between family time, so I could live up to those words. It is from the legacy of those words that many books will be generated.

First, I would like to acknowledge my four beautiful children, who made me who I am today. All four of them were given to me by God; they were not accidents or mistakes. Although I was a young mother and had no idea what my future would be, I consented to every single conception, despite the outside thoughts of others, because I knew all of them had a God-given purpose. Although the stigma of having them with different fathers stuck with me and I was labelled as being confused, unstable and too young to have children, each of them is significant in my life, helping me to be the person I am today: shaped, defined, stable, purposeful and important. They continue to ensure I progress to be a better version of myself by reminding me that I am a great mother and that they appreciate and love me. Though they might also express that they had it hard as children, they also remind me that it was also good and I did my best to give them the best with what we had. So, my four legends are the reasons I hold onto my life and keep pushing for the best. This includes my five grandchildren, who will individually be great, powerful entrepreneurs, doing what I have never done and achieving more than their parents' aspirations and achievements.

I acknowledge my parents, who brought me into this world and who stuck together for 46 years in marriage. They both inspired me to believe that being married is important and although I had broken relationships, in my mind, I wanted to be like them and be married and have a family. In spite of my mess, they were always my inspiration that marriage can work and to give me the hope that I would one day be married, settled and happy for real. I thank God for their lives and for being there for my children and me through my ups and downs and for loving me even when my life looked messy. Rather than judge me or shut me out when I had my children out of wedlock, they still respected me and believed in my dream that I would one day be the nurse I had told my mum I would be at the age of five.

Thank you to my husband, who entered my life at the beginning of my waiting journey, who believed in me and knew I was worth the wait, who put up with my late nights of writing, who prayed me through completing my book and who loved my past, present and future. Not only did he express love, but he also showed me love. He knew my worth and respected where I was and where I was going and he continued to stand by me, pushing me to the forefront, putting his dreams and visions on hold until mine had been completed.

Thank you to my family and friends, too many names to list. You know who you are, those who supported, helped, encouraged and inspired me throughout my life's journeys. Thank you to me for believing in my future, seeing another reflection in the mirror, changing me for me and loving me first so I could love my family and friends, making things that once looked miserable look achievable. I was finally on the road to winning and you all made it possible. Thank you all with a special love. Keep dreaming, believing and pushing for greatness and always remember that all things are possible despite your past.

Dedications

Family, Friends and Mentors

I dedicate this book to Ten, Ren, Den and Jen, my four heroes — they know why their names are shortened; it's an inside, family joke. Each of them has inspired me with who they have become or are becoming. My son, Deniro, has become a husband, and a wonderful father to my beautiful granddaughter and an entrepreneur, who continues to create value, he his creative, speaks with intellect and wisdom, he kind and absolutely hilarious. I love being in his presence, especially when I need a good belly laugh and if I were his little brother or sister, I would say that I wanted to be like him when I grew up.

To Tenisha (my beautiful bun-bun), my oldest daughter: I am so proud of you and the woman into which you've developed. In spite of raising my beautiful grandchildren as a single parent, you have proven that you can be more than a statistic. I have seen you evolve into a businesswoman and entrepreneur, managing your children and home life and still have the capacity to work at your personal business, always giving your children the best and constantly pushing to pursue all your dreams. Keep pushing, as your best is yet to come.

To Renece, my twin: you are beautiful, in and out. You're so mini-me and I am so proud of you as you've pushed for a career in nursing like me. It is not easy juggling a home life, studying and running your own business. And to top it off, you are a great mother for my beautiful grandchildren. Your determination has really inspired me even as you embark on your new career, keep pushing for greatness; your best days are ahead of you.

Finally, to my belly-wash, my singer, my writer, my teacher and my prayer partner, my JJ squad: Jenae, I know you wanted a little brother as you were bored being alone as the only child at home, but in a couple of years' time, you will love the idea that you're not looking after your little brother when you want to go out with your friends. Trust me; you won't regret being the last child. Jenae, you are beautiful, encouraging, kind, thoughtful and inspirational and I want to be like you when I grow up and be on your JJ squad team. One day, you will be on TV, showing the world your beautiful voice. Keep singing and believing in yourself and don't give up on your dreams. I know you will make mummy proud one day.

To all of my nieces and nephews: Auntie Mel loves each one of you very much. To all of my sisters-in-law, too many names to list: you are all beautiful and I am glad to call you my sisters.

To all of my stepchildren, near and far and to my godchildren: I love you all dearly.

To my loving parents, Deloris and Collin Harrison, the two anchors that keep our family together, who would give up their lives for us, who have always been there for me, embracing me with their love and kindness. My mother, who has no filter and tells it like it is but then loves on you with the words, 'I just want the best for my children.' My father, who is always smiling with that famous Harrison smile, always cooking — the number one chef — and going out of his way for everyone.

To my Auntie Enid, my godmother who died while writing this book, who was one of my biggest supporters, who made me feel right even when I was wrong and who never judged me — she was the person I trusted with my life and I am so lost without her, but her memory has pushed me to continue to write. I can hear her now: 'A book?' and giving me her contagious laugh.

To all of my brothers: me being the only girl of seven, growing up with you all, I felt protected, loved and spoilt. It somewhat caused me to be strong and bold because I felt like I had an army behind me. Thank you all for the surrounding love.

To Nicole and Sharon, my big and little sisters, known as Niks and Shaz who both moved from being friends to having the honour of being my sisters. They never gave up on me, through the good, the bad and the ugly. Both have played the role of being my sisters with no walls and no barriers. They have been my shoulders to cry on, my advisers, my counsellors, my confidants, my prayer warriors and my true and loyal friends.

To Toni Kelly, aka TK, my tweenie, my laughing partner, my sister from another mister, my miss transparent: it was her story and testimony that inspired me to be open and transparent, pushing me to take off my mask and be myself.

To Lisa, who I met at church over 20 years ago, who loved my children as their auntie: she is beautiful inside and out. Although we don't see much of each other, she will always have a special place in my heart for her kindness and always being there when I need her and I am sorry that life has pulled us apart.

To Sheila, who I only started building a friendship with just six years ago, but it feels as if I have known her much longer. She came into my life during my journey of finding love and she inspired me to be what a wife should be, standing with me so that one day I would find love, preparing me with her encouragement and wise words and making me laugh when I wanted to give up on loving.

To Dahna-esther, who came into my life at the end of my studying for my degree, who prayed me through it, who reminded me that I was enough and that I could dream again!

To Bishop John Francis, the 'man of faith' I mirrored to pursue my crazy faith: every messaged he preached kept me believing by faith. Even when all odds were against me, his messages on faith inspired me, that all things were possible if we believe. The encouragement he gave me, stating that it was not too late to go back to school and become a nurse, every time I reflected on: 'it's not too late', I would continue to push to complete my career. Thank you.

To Dr Rachael-Rose, who mentored me from afar, who was my teacher in Bible school, who pushed me in Bible school, encouraged me to write great assignments and marked my assignments with A+: It was the beginning of my student's journey and it was those marks that pushed me to believe in myself that although I was a high school dropout, I still had the capacity to achieve and that it was possible to go back to study.

To Elder Paulette Kerr, who believed in my leadership, instilling me with values and being a great leader, who grounded me in my faith, who mothered me in my walk with Christ: you supported me and even when I dropped out, you reigned me back in with love and reminding me of my purpose. Thank you for mentoring me.

To my new pastors, Pastor Mike and Donna-Marie White. When I started a new journey with Christ at their ministry, I knew I had a second chance to start over again; a new start, new environment and new opportunities. When I first heard one of Pastor Mike's messages, I knew that I was strategically positioned in their ministry as judging by the realness and relatable engagement he had with the crowd, I knew he would get the realness of my book. Thank you both for embracing me and instilling a mindset re-set in my new journey.

To my brother, Nicholas, aka Von Mozar, who was the first in my family to become an author, writing *Ignorance Kills* and many more books after that and who continues to strive to become a bestselling author: his passion for writing inspired me to start writing only later to find out that our great-granduncle was also a writer. I knew then that it was in our DNA to be great writers. Thank you, Nicky, for setting the pathway for our family to create new and great young writers, including my youngest daughter, Jenae, who was inspired to write and who was chosen and featured in a book for first-time writers. Mummy is so proud of you.

To all of my friends. Each person has played a different role in my journey, but they were significant to the plan. You all had an impact on my journey, giving me love, encouragement, commitment and friendship. Some of you saw tears, laughter and jokes, some of you supported my children and me and some just listened and advised — thank you all for playing a role in my life. You are all my friends for life. And my famous phrase, that I normally say is: 'Don't lie, is it.' To all of my friends who I have not individually mentioned — you know who you are — and to all of my family, near and far, including my heavenly family. Thank you.

To all of my exes and the naysayers: you also played a role in my journey. Every pain and hurt you inflicted only pushed me to be better and to become a beautiful treasure — one man's trash is another man's treasure.

To my husband, Mr Martin (Stevie-baby), my 'I will do anything for you' who keeps me grounded and stable as his wife, leader and mother, who values my future and who allows me to be myself without adding to it or taking away from it. He speaks the life and wisdom of our future. His strength is communication and his weakness is that he allows me to talk, but he still knows how to lead his family and he has gained his respect as my husband. Thank you for loving me; you are amazing.

Finally, to God, my first love, my everything: thank you for trusting me, for choosing me to complete each journey and for the strength you give me when I feel like giving up and throwing in the towel. Each time you reminded me of my promise, my worth and the greatness of my comeback; therefore, I dedicate this book especially to you.

Works Cited

1. Boyd, Evelyn M. and Ann W. Fales. 'Reflective Learning: Key to Learning From Experience'. *Sage Journals: Journal of Humanistic Psychology*, 1 April 1983, https://doi.org/10.1177/0022167883232011.

2. 'Causes — Clinical Depression'. *NHS*, 2019, https://www.nhs.uk/mental-health/conditions/clinical-depression/causes/. Accessed 29 April 2021.

3. Gray, Madison J. 'Depression: The Other Side of "Man Up"'. *Newsone*, 6 June 2014, https://newsone.com/3016305/black-male-depression/. Accessed 29 April 2021.

4. 'Overview — Clinical Depression'. *NHS*, 2019, https://www.nhs.uk/mental-health/conditions/clinicaldepression/overview/#:~:text=Life%2Dchanging%20events%2C%20such%20as,depressed%20for%20no%20obvious%20reason. Accessed 29 April 2021.

5. Pickens, Josie. 'Depression and the Black Superwoman Syndrome'. *Ebony*, 13 November, 2017, https://www.ebony.com/health/depression-black-superwoman-syndrome-real/. Accessed 29 April 2021.

Conscious Dreams
PUBLISHING

Be the author of your own destiny

www.consciousdreamspublishing.com

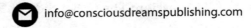
info@consciousdreamspublishing.com

Let's connect

CPSIA information can be obtained
at www.ICGtesting.com
Printed in the USA
LVHW081750180522
719025LV00013B/340